Venice Observed

Books by Mary McCarthy

Ideas and the Novel
Cannibals and Missionaries
The Mask of State: Watergate Portraits
The Seventeenth Degree
Birds of America
The Writing on the Wall
Mary McCarthy's Theatre Chronicles
The Group
On the Contrary
The Stones of Florence
Venice Observed
Memories of a Catholic Girlhood
A Charmed Life
The Groves of Academe
Cast a Cold Eye
The Oasis
The Company She Keeps

Mary McCarthy

Venice Observed

A Harvest/HBJ Book
Harcourt Brace Jovanovich, Publishers
San Diego   New York   London

This edition, 1963, is published by arrangement with the author and with rights reserved by the author, and comprises the text of an edition published in 1956 that included both text and illustrations. Some of the text in this book originally appeared, in different form, in
The New Yorker

ISBN 0-15-693521-X   (Harvest/HBJ : pbk.)

Printed in the United States of America

L M N O P Q

Contents

I

Venice Preserved

'Venice at 8 to 9; went to Danielli's [*sic*]. Saw St Mark's, the Piazza, the Grand Canal and some churches: fine day – very picturesque – general effect fine – individual things not.' Herbert Spencer in his diary, 1880.

'*Il disoit l'avoir trouvée autre qu'il ne l'avoit imaginée, et un peu moins admirable . . . La police, la situation, l'arsenal, la place de S. Marc, et la presse des peuples étrangiers lui semblarent les choses plus remerquables.*' Michel de Montaigne in his *Journal du Voyage en Italie*, 1580-81.

The rationalist mind has always had its doubts about Venice. The watery city receives a dry inspection, as though it were a myth for the credulous – poets and honeymooners. Montaigne, his servant recorded, '*n'y trouva pas cete fameuse beauté qu'on attribue aus dames de Venise, et si vid les plus nobles de celles qui en font traffique.*' That famous beauty – the Frenchman sceptically sought it among the vaunted courtesans, who numbered 11,654 at the time of his visit. He had supper with the pearl of them all, no. 204

in the Catalogue of the Chief and Most Honoured Courtesans of Venice. '*Le lundi à souper, 6 de novembre, la Signora Veronica Franco, janti fame venitiane, envoia vers lui pour lui presenter un petit livre de Lettres qu'elle a composé.*' It was evidently a literary evening. This Aspasia, at thirty-four, was retired from her profession and kept a salon frequented by poets and painters; she composed sonnets and letters and terza rima verses and had it in mind to write an epic poem. Henry III had visited her and brought back a report of her to France, together with two of her sonnets. But Montaigne was more impressed by the police and the high cost of living. '*Les vivres y sont chers come à Paris.*'

That famous beauty – three hundred years later, the British philosopher, a bachelor, cocked a dubious eye at it in the touted palazzi. Everywhere he detected a 'striving' for the picturesque. He was particularly unimpressed by the leading examples: the little, leaning Palazzo Dario, in the Lombard style, with insets of porphyry and verd-antique, the Corner-Spinelli, by Mauro Coducci, with its remarkable balconies, and the Ca' Rezzonico, the baroque grey-columned prodigy begun by Longhena, in which the poet Browning was shortly to die. The Doge's Palace exasperated Spencer to the point where he felt it necessary to hint bluntly at some general principles of architecture: 'Dumpy arches of the lower tier of the Ducal Palace and the dumpy windows in the wall above ... the meaningless diaper pattern covering this wall, which suggests something woven rather than built; and the long row of projections and spikes surmounting the coping, which remind one of nothing so much as the vertebral spines of a fish.' So much for the Doge's Palace. 'And what about St Mark's? Well, I admit that it is a fine sample of barbaric architecture.'

Among Venice's spells is one of peculiar potency: the power to awaken the philistine dozing in the sceptic's breast. People of this kind – dry, prose people of superior intelligence – object to feeling what they are supposed to feel, in the presence of marvels. They wish to feel something else. The extreme of this position is to feel nothing. Such a case was Stendhal's; Venice left him cold. He was there only a short time and departed with barely a comment to pursue an intrigue in Padua. Another lover of Italy, D. H. Lawrence (on one side of his nature, a debunker, a plain home-truth teller like Ruskin before him), put down his first reaction in a poem: 'Abhorrent green, slippery city, Whose Doges were old and had ancient eyes . . .' And Gibbon 'was afforded some hours of astonishment and some days of disgust by the spectacle of Venice.'

This grossly advertised wonder, this gold idol with clay feet, this *trompe-l'oeil*, this painted deception, this cliché – what intelligent iconoclast could fail to experience a destructive impulse in her presence? Ruskin, who was her overdue Jeremiah, and who came in the end to detest nearly everything in Venice, spent half his days trying to expose her frauds – climbing ladders in dusty churches to prove (what he had long suspected) that the Venetian Renaissance was a false front, a cynical trick, that the sleeping Doge Vendramin, for example, in marble effigy, atop his tomb in SS. Giovanni and Paolo was only a carven profile turned to the public: the other side, the side turned away from the public, being a vacancy, a featureless slab. Napoleon, Stendhal's hero, went the whole way in brutal forthrightness, when he announced to the Venetian envoys, sent to treat diplomatically, his intention of shattering the image: 'I have 80,000 men and twenty gunboats; *io non voglio più Inquisitori, non voglio più Senato; sarò un Attila per lo stato Veneto.*'

Io non voglio – a rude form of the verb, to wish. The phrase rings out, brazen, prophesying pillage: the sack of St Mark's treasury, the rape of pictures for the Louvre, the agate-eyed, winged lion wrenched from his column on the quay to be carted off to the Invalides, the bronze horses of Nero hauled down from St Mark's balcony to wait in front of the Tuileries until they could grace an arch of triumph on the Place du Carrousel.

The lion, damaged, came back. The horses came back. Their rape and return form simply another anecdote in the repertory of the guides of Venice, who drone it out in French, English and German, each to his flock of tourists herded in the Piazza between the three standards, where, on the eve of Napoleon's appearance, the Tree of Liberty stood and a woman friend of Byron's, the Countess Querini-Benzoni, *la biondina in gondoleta*, danced round it, dressed only in an Athenian tunic.

Napoleon's prophecy came true, though not altogether in the sense he meant. He did become another Attila for Venice, that is, a figure in its touristic legend, another discountenanced invader, like the Genoese at Chioggia, like Pepin, whose army was engulfed in the lagoons and perished, according to tradition, as the Egyptians did in the Red Sea. Attila opened the story; refugees, fleeing from him on the mainland, sought safety on the fishing islets and began to build their improbable city, houses of wattles and twigs set on piles driven into the mud, 'like sea-birds' nests,' wrote Cassiodorus, secretary of Theodoric, 'half on sea and half on land and spread like the Cyclades over the surface of the waters.' Napoleon closed the story, as he closed in the Piazza San Marco with the Fabbrica Nuova at the end, giving them – both square and narrative – their final, necessary form.

Without Napoleon, Venice would not be complete. Without Napoleon, the last Doge, Lodovico Manin (looking very much like a despondent housemaid in his portrait in the Museo Correr), could not have handed the ducal *corno*, tearfully, to a servant, saying, 'I won't be needing this any more.' A pithy statement, in the matter-of-fact tradition of the noble Romans, from whom the Venetians claimed descent. And on the plebeian level, thanks to Napoleon, a gondolier had the last laugh. Examining Napoleon's proclamation, which showed the armorial lion holding the Book, in which the old inscription, *Pax tibi, Marce, Evangelista meus*, was replaced by 'The Rights of Men and Citizens,' the gondolier is supposed to have commented, 'At last he's turned the page.'

But from Napoleon's point of view, surely, that was just the trouble with Venice – the increment of childish history, of twice-told tales. The ducal bonnet, the Inquisitors, the Bocca del Leone, into which anonymous denunciations were slipped, the Doge's golden umbrella, the Bucintoro, the Marriage of the Adriatic, the Ring, the Bridge of Sighs, Casanova, the Leads, Shylock, the Rialto, Titian, Tintoretto, *les dames de Venise*, the capture of the Body of St Mark, Lepanto, the pigeons, the pirates, the Taking of Constantinople, with the blind Doge Dandolo at ninety-five leading the attack, Marco Polo, the Queen of Cyprus, and (still yet to come!) Byron on the Lido on horseback, Byron swimming the Grand Canal, 'Julian and Maddalo,' Byron in the Armenian convent, Wagner in the Piazzà listening to *Tannhäuser* played by the Austrian band; Wagner in the Palazzo Vendramin, Browning, D'Annunzio, Duse, and finally, last and first, the gondola, the eternal gondola, with its steel prow and its witty gondolier – to a 'new man,' a leveller, what insufferable tedium, what a stagnant canal-stench must have emanated from all this. '*Non voglio più.*' When he announced that he would be an Attila, Napoleon's irritation cannot have been purely political; it must have been an impatience, not so much with an obsolete, reactionary form of government, not so much even with the past (he was awed by the Sphinx and the Pyramids), as with an eternal present, with a city that had become a series of souvenirs and 'views.'

Henry James, a lover of Venice, was familiar with the sensation. 'The Venice of today is a vast museum where the little wicket that admits you is perpetually turning and creaking, and you march through the institution with a herd of fellow-gazers. There is nothing left to discover or describe, and originality of attitude is utterly impossible.' After two weeks, he said, you began to feel as restless as though you were on shipboard, the Piazza figuring 'as an enormous saloon and the Riva degli Schiavoni as a promenade deck.'

No stones are so trite as those of Venice, that is, precisely, so well worn. It has been part museum, part amusement park, living off the entrance fees of tourists, ever since the early eighteenth century, when its former sources of revenue ran dry. The carnival that lasted half a year was not just a spontaneous expression of Venetian license; it was a calculated tourist attraction. Francesco Guardi's early 'views' were the postcards of that period. In the Venetian preserve, a thick bitter-sweet marmalade, tourism itself became a spicy ingredient, suited to the foreign taste; legends of dead tourists now are boiled up daily by gondoliers and guides. Byron's desk, Gautier's palace, Ruskin's boarding house, the room where Browning died, Barbara Hutton's plate-glass window – these memorabilia replace the Bucintoro or Paolo Sarpi's statue as objects of interest. The Venetian crafts have become sideshows – glass-blowing, bead-stringing, lace-making; you watch the product made, like pink spun sugar at a circus, and bring a sample home, as a souvenir. Venetian manufactures today lay no claim to beauty or elegance, only to being 'Venetian.'

And there is no use pretending that the tourist Venice is not the real Venice, which is possible with other cities – Rome or Florence or Naples. The tourist Venice *is* Venice: the gondolas, the sunsets, the changing light, Florian's, Quadri's, Torcello, Harry's Bar, Murano, Burano, the pigeons, the glass beads, the vaporetto. Venice is a folding picture-post-card of itself. And though it is true (as is sometimes said, sententiously) that nearly two hundred thousand people live their ordinary working lives in Venice, they too exist in it as tourists or guides. Nearly every Venetian is an art-appreciator, a connoisseur of Venice, ready to talk of Tintoretto or to show you, at his own suggestion, the spiral staircase (said to challenge the void), to demonstrate the Venetian dialect or identify the sound of the Marangona, the bell of the Campanile, when it rings out at midnight.

A count shows the Tiepolo on the ceiling of his wife's bedroom; a dentist shows his sitting-room, which was formerly a ridotto. Everything has been catalogued, with a pride that is more in the knowledge than in the thing itself. 'A fake,' genially says a gentleman, pointing to his Tintoretto. 'Réjane's,' says a house-owner, pointing to the broken-down bed in the apartment she wants to let. The vanity of displaying knowledge can outweigh commercial motives or the vanity of ownership. 'Eighteenth century?' you say hopefully to an antique-dealer, as you look at a set of china. 'No, nineteenth,' he answers with firmness, losing the sale. In my apartment, I wish everything to be Venetian, but 'No,' says the landlady, as I ask about a cabinet: 'Florentine.' We stare at a big enthroned Madonna in the bedroom – very bad. She would like me to think it a Bellini and she measures the possibility against the art knowledge she estimates me to possess. '*School* of Giovanni Bellini,' she announces, nonchalantly, extricating herself from the dilemma.

A Venetian nobleman has made a study of plants peculiar to Venice and shows slides on a projector. He has a library of thirty thousand volumes, mainly devoted to Venetian history. In the public libraries, in the wintertime the same set of loungers pores over Venetian archives or illustrated books on Venetian art; they move from the Correr library, when it closes, to the heatless Marciana, where they sit huddled in their overcoats, and finally to the Querini-Stampaglia, which stays open until late at night.

The Venetians catalogue everything, including themselves. 'These grapes are brown,' I complain to the young vegetable-dealer in Santa Maria Formosa. 'What is wrong with that? *I* am brown,' he replies. 'I am the housemaid of the painter Vedova,' says a maid, answering the telephone. 'I am a Jew,' begins a cross-eyed stranger who is next in line in a bakeshop. 'Would you care to see the synagogue?'

Almost any Venetian, even a child, will abandon whatever he is doing in order to show you something. They do not merely give directions; they lead, or in some cases follow, to make sure you are still on the right way. Their great fear is that you will miss an artistic or 'typical' sight. A sacristan, who has already been tipped, will not let you leave until you have seen the last Palma Giovane. The 'pope' of the Chiesa dei Greci calls up to his housekeeper to throw his black hat out the window and settles it firmly on his broad brow so that he can lead us personally to the Archaeological Museum in the Piazza San Marco; he is afraid that, if he does not see to it, we shall miss the Greek statuary there.

This is Venetian courtesy. Foreigners who have lived here a long time dismiss it with the observation: 'They have nothing else to do.' But idleness here is alert, on the *qui vive* for the opportunity of sightseeing; nothing delights a born Venetian so much as a free gondola ride. When the funeral gondola, a great black-and-gold ornate hearse, draws up beside a fondamenta, it is an occasion for aesthetic pleasure. My neighbourhood was especially favoured in this way, because across the campo was the Old Men's Home. Everyone has noticed the Venetian taste in shop-displays, which extends down to the poorest bargeman, who cuts his watermelons in half and shows them, pale pink, with green rims against the green side-canal, in which a pink palace with oleanders is reflected. *Che bello, che magnifico, che luce, che colore!* – they are all *professori delle Belle Arti.* And throughout the Veneto, in the old Venetian possessions, this internal tourism, this expertise, is rife. In Bassano, at the Civic Museum, I took the Mayor for the local art-critic until he interrupted his discourse on the jewel-tones ('like Murano glass') in the Bassani pastorals to look at his watch and cry out: 'My citizens are calling me.' Nearby, in a Palladian villa, a Venetian lady suspired, '*Ah, bellissima,*' on being shown a hearthstool in the shape of a life-size stuffed leather pig. Harry's Bar has a drink called a Tiziano, made of grape-fruit juice and champagne and coloured pink with grenadine or bitters. 'You ought to have a Tintoretto,' someone remonstrated, and the proprietor regretted that he had not yet invented that drink, but he had a Bellini and a Giorgione.

When the Venetians stroll out in the evening, they do not avoid the Piazza San Marco, where the tourists are, as the Romans do with Doney's on the Via Veneto. The Venetians go to look at the tourists, and the tourists look back at them. It is all for the ear and eye, this city, but primarily for the eye. Built on water, it is an endless succession of reflections and echoes, a mirroring. Con-trary to popular belief, there are no back canals where a tourist will not meet himself, with a camera, in the person of the other tourist crossing the little bridge. And no word can be spoken in this city that is not an echo of something said before. '*Mais c'est aussi cher que Paris!*' exclaims a Frenchman in a restaurant, unaware that he repeats Mon-taigne. The complaint against foreigners, voiced by a foreigner, chimes querulously through the ages, in unison with the medieval monk who found St Mark's Square filled with 'Turks, Libyans, Parthians, and other monsters of the sea.' Today it is the Germans we complain of, and no doubt they complain of the Americans, in the same words.

Nothing can be said here (including this statement) *that has not been said before.* One often hears the Piazza described as an open-air drawing room; the observation goes back to Napoleon, who called it 'the best drawing-room in Europe.' A friend likens the ornamental coping of St Mark's to sea foam, but Ruskin thought of this first: '... at last, as if in ecstasy, the crests of the arches break into a marbly foam, and toss themselves far into the blue sky in flashes and wreaths of sculptured spray...' Another friend observes that the gondolas are like hearses; I was struck by the novelty of the fancy until I found it, two days later, in Shelley: 'that funereal bark.' Now I find it everywhere. A young man, boarding the vaporetto, sighs that 'Venice is so urban,' a remark which at least *sounds* original and doubtless did when Proust spoke of the 'always urban impression' made by Venice in the midst of the sea. And the worst of it is that nearly all these clichés are true. It is true, for example, that St Mark's at night looks like a painted stage flat; this is a fact which everybody notices and which everybody thinks he has discovered for himself. I blush to remember the sound of my own voice, clear in its own conceit, enunciating this proposition in the Piazza, nine years ago.

'I envy you, writing about Venice,' says the newcomer. 'I pity you,' says the old hand. One thing is certain. Sophistication, that modern kind of sophistication that begs to differ, to be paradoxical, to invert, is not a possible attitude in Venice. In time, this becomes the beauty of the place. One gives up the struggle and submits to a classic experience. One accepts the fact that what one is about to feel or say has not only been said before by Goethe or Musset but is on the tip of the tongue of the tourist from Iowa who is alighting in the Piazzetta with his wife in her furpiece and jewelled pin. Those Others, the existential enemy, are here identical with oneself. After a time in Venice, one comes to look with pity on the efforts of the newcomer to disassociate himself from the crowd. He has found a 'little' church – has he? – quite off the beaten track, a real gem, with inlaid coloured marbles on a soft dove grey, like a jewel box. He means Santa Maria dei Miracoli. As you name it, his face falls. It is so well known, then? Or has he the notion of counting the lions that look down from the window ledges of the palazzi? They remind him of cats. Has anybody ever noticed how many cats there are in Venice or compared them to the lions? On my table two books lie open with chapters on the Cats of Venice. My face had fallen too when I came upon them in the house of an old bookseller, for I too had dared think that I had hold of an original perception.

The cat = the lion. Venice is a kind of pun on itself, which is another way of saying that it is a mirror held up to its own shimmering image – the central conceit on which it has evolved. The Grand Canal is in the shape of a fish (or an eel, if you wish to be more literal); on the Piazzetta, St Theodore rides the crocodile (or the fish, if you prefer). Dolphins and scallop shells carry out the theme in decoration. It becomes frozen in the state ceremonial; the Doge weds the Adriatic in a mock, i.e., a punning, marriage. The lion enters the state myth in the company of the Evangelist and begets litter on litter of lions – all allusions, half jesting, half literary, to the original one: the great War Lion of the Arsenal gate whose Book ('Peace be with you') is ominously closed, the graduated lions from Greece below him, in front of the Arsenal, like the three bears in the story, the King of Beasts with uplifted tail in *trompe-l'œil* on the Scuola di San Marco, the red, roaring lions on the left of St Mark's who play hobbyhorse for children every day, the lion of Chioggia, which Venetians say is only a cat, the doggy lion of the Porta della Carta being honored by the Doge Foscari . . . From St Mark's Square, they spread out, in varying shapes and sizes, whiskered or clean-shaven, through Venice and her ancient territories, as far as Nauplia in the Peloponnesus. But St Mark's lion is winged, i.e., a monster, and this produces a whole crop of monsters, basilisks and dragons, with their attendant saints and slayers, all dear to Venetian artists. St Jerome, thanks to his tame lion, becomes a favourite saint of the Venetians.

The twinning continues. The great pink church of the Frari is echoed on the other side of the city by the great pink church of the Dominicans, the other preaching order. And in St Mark's shelter, near the Pietra del Bando, four small identical brothers, called the Moors, in porphyry embrace two and two, like orphans. The famous Venetian *trompe-l'œil*, marble stimulating brocade or flat simulating round, is itself a sort of twinning or unending duplication, as with a repeating decimal.

Venice is a game (see how many lions you can count; E. V. Lucas found 75 on the Porta della Carta alone), a fantasy, a fable, a city of Methuselahs, in which mortality has almost been vanquished. Titian, according to the old writers, was carried off by the plague in his hundredth year. How many Venetian painters can you count who, like him, passed three score and ten before they were gathered to their fathers? Jacopo Bellini (70 years), Gentile Bellini (78), Giovanni Bellini (86), Lorenzo Lotto (76), Tintoretto (76), Palma Il Giovane (84), Tiepolo (80), G.D. Tiepolo (77), Pietro Longhi (83), Alessandro Longhi (80), Piazzetta (71), Canaletto (71), Guardi (81). And among the sculptors and architects, Pietro Lombardo (65), Sansovino (93), Alessandro Vittoria (83), Palladio (72), Longhena (84). This makes Venice, the nourisher of old men, appear as a dream, the Fountain of Youth which Ponce de Leon sought in the New World. It brings us back to the rationalist criticism of Venice, as a myth that ought to be exploded.

'Those Pantaloons,' a French ambassador called the Venetian statesmen in the early seventeenth century, when the astuteness of their diplomacy was supposed to be the wonder of Europe. The capacity to arouse contempt and disgust in the onlooker was a natural concomitant, not only of Venice's prestige, but of the whole fairy tale she wove about herself; her Council of Ten, her mysterious three Inquisitors, her dungeons, her punishments, 'swift, silent, and sure.' Today, we smile a little at the fairy tale of Venetian history, at the doge under his golden umbrella, as we smile at the nuns entertaining their admirers in Guardi's picture in the Ca' Rezzonico, at the gaming tables and the masks; it is the same smile we give to the all-woman regatta, to the graduated lions, to Carpaccio's man-eating dragon. If we shiver as we pass through the Leads or as we slip our hand into the Bocca del Leone, it is a histrionic shiver, partly self-induced, like the screams that ring out from the little cars in an amusement-park tunnel as they shoot past the waxworks. For us, Venetian history is a curio; those hale old doges and warriors seem to us a strange breed of sea-animal who left behind them the pink, convoluted shell they grew to protect them, which is Venice.

The old historians took a different line and tended to view Venice as an allegory in which vice and reckless greed (or undemocratic government) met their just reward. They held up Venice as a cautionary example to other nations. But we cannot feel this moral indignation or this solemn awe before the Venetian spectacle. In Ravenna or Mantua, we can sense the gloom of history steal over us like a real shadow. These cities are truly sad, and they compel belief in the crimes and tragedies that were enacted in them. Venice remains a child's pageant, minute and ingenious, brightened with touches of humorous 'local colour,' as in the pageant pictures of Gentile Bellini and Carpaccio. Or, with Tintoretto and Veronese, it swells into a bepearled myth. The sumptuous Apotheoses of the rooms of the Doge's Palace, the blues and golds and nacreous flesh tones, discredit the reality of the Turkish disasters that were befalling the Republic at the time they were painted, just as Giorgione's idylls discredit the reality of the League of Cambrai. With the eighteenth-century painters, the pneumatic goddess is deflated. The pictures of Canaletto and Guardi and Longhi take us back again into playland, with toy boats (the gondolas) and dominos and masks and lacy shawls, while the pictures of Tiepolo with their chalky tones take us to a circus, in which everyone is a clown or a trapeze artist, in white theatrical make-up and theatrical costuming. Napoleon was at the gates, but it is hard to believe it. It was hard for the Venetians, at the time. For them, their 'liberation' from the oligarchy was simply another pageant, another procession, with allegorical figures in costume before the old stage flat of St Mark's, which was hung with garlands and draperies. At the opera that night, the fall of the Republic was celebrated by a ballet danced by the workers of the Arsenal; the patricians were there, in silks and laces and brocades, gold and silver lamés, diamonds and pearls, and, in honour of the occasion, gondoliers were admitted free.

Everything that happens in Venice has this inherent improbability, of which the gondola, floating, insubstantial, at once romantic and haunting, charming and absurd, is the symbol. 'Why don't they put outboard motors on them?' an American wondered, looking on the practical side. But a dream is only practical in unexpected ways; that is, it is *resourceful*, like the Venetians. 'It is another world,' people say, noting chiefly the absence of the automobile. And it *is* another world, a palpable fiction, in which the unexpected occurs with regularity; that is why it hovers on the brink of humour.

A prominent nobleman this autumn, rushing to the sickbed of a friend, slipped getting into his motorboat and fell into the Grand Canal. All Venice laughed. But if the count had had his misadventure in Padua, on *terra ferma*, if he had fallen getting out of his car, everyone would have condoled with him. Traffic lights are not funny, but it is funny to have one in Venice over a canal-intersection. The same with the Venetian fire brigade. The things of *this* world reveal their essential absurdity when they are put in the Venetian context. In the unreal realm of the canals, as in a Swiftian Lilliput, the real world, with its contrivances, appears as a vast folly.

2

The Loot

The signore and the signora were separated for tax purposes, explained the real-estate agent. '*J'ai une bonne place pour vous*,' he had told me, a few days before, as he led me along a fondamenta, jingling a set of house keys. The apartment was very pretty: four large rooms overlooking the garden of a palazzo and furnished, for the most part, in a gay Venetian rococo, blue-and-white stripes, pink rosebuds, cabinets painted in the manner of Tiepolo, chairs with scallop-shell backs. But now I wanted to know precisely how many persons were going to occupy the apartment above, sharing a common entrance-hall and a bathtub with me – 'only when you are out,' the agent had hastily stipulated. 'You do not have to worry; they do not take many baths.' I had accepted this reassurance, joining rather thinly in his crackling laugh. The signora, he went on, would have her own washbowl and toilet and kitchenette in the quarters she was fixing for herself upstairs. She and her teen-age daughter and son would take most of their meals at the grandmother's. This son had not been specified in the original invoice; he had transpired as the deal progressed. And only the night before, I had been told by a Venetian acquaintance that there was a signore too and had him pointed out to me as he was leaving a restaurant – a dark, red-fleshed man with an oiled moustache. 'You did not *say* there was a husband!' I now reproached the real-estate agent in his office, pushing the lease aside. 'He will not be at home; you will not see him,' the agent promised. For tax reasons, the signore had a separate domicile, over the Taverna La Fenice. '*Madame et vous*,' the agent applied his pet formula, like a soothing lotion, '*serez des bonnes amies.*' 'I *hope* so,' I retorted darkly. The speciality of this little man, I had discovered, seemed to be renting apartments that were already occupied. He had begun by trying to rent me his own apartment, with himself in it. '*Des bonnes amies*,' he now repeated, and I took out my fountain pen and signed.

Contrary to everyone's predictions, it has not worked out badly. The agent was right when he reiterated. '*C'est une bonne place pour vous, Madame.*' The signora is a tall ash-blonde string-bean of a woman, with a long droll, Modigliani face – a good-natured, feckless comedian, the 'second' female part in a Goldoni play, who scolds and winks as she slaps about with her dustcloth, a cigarette hanging from one corner of her mouth. And it is true; I do not see the signore, though he sleeps here, I find, after all. Lying in their matrimonial bed – a vast Florentine gilt affair of the cinquecento with life-size Cupids, more like a barge than a bed – I hear his step on the stair, late at night, as he ascends with the signora after a supper at the Mamma's or at the Colomba restaurant. In the mornings, I

sometimes hear his voice raised in anger, in a matrimonial
dispute, or I catch a glimpse of a pair of pomaded moustaches disappearing out the door, followed by a flash of
svelte polo-coat. But that is all he is to me: a stormy,
uxorious voice, a whisk of moustache and coat-tails, a
surreptitious step on the stair. Like Jove, he visits his
premises by stealth, and I come to think of him as simply
a male totem, a bull or a shower of coins. He is gone by
eight in the morning. The signora says he is in the con-
struction business and is putting up some houses near San
Giobbe. They have come down in the world – like
nearly everyone in Venice. I can see this from their
wedding photograph, which hangs beside my bed. They
are standing by the Grand Canal, with the Dogana and
the Salute in the background; the signore, thinner and
paler, with a mere sketch of his present moustache, wears
a morning coat and striped trousers; the signora is in white
satin, with veil and pearls and orange blossoms. The
picture is over-exposed, which gives it a filmy sadness,
fully justified by subsequent events. He was a *dottore delle
Belle Arti*, the signora tells me, and he lists himself in the
telephone book as 'Professor Giuliano.' For ten years, says
the signora, they have not got along together. '*Ah, Elva,
Elva!*' she commiserates with herself, yawning. '*Poverina.*'

The signora is a matter-of-fact person, shrewd, candid,
and naive. With her long face, fair hair, and wide-set,
almost Mongoloid, rolling blue-green eyes, she seems to
me a true daughter of Venice, which in fact she is. The
signore, whom I do not care for, I decide to classify as

southern. Dottore delle Belle Arti or not, he is too coarse-grained and swart to be a real Venetian. It is only his marital situation ('separated for tax purposes') that seems to have been inspired by the playful genius loci. There is much wry humour in Venice and very little pretence. There is no syrup either, nothing cloying or gluey; the gondolier's taut, erect pose sets the pattern. Where Naples is operatic, Venice is chamber music or, if you wish, Mozartian opera – Leporello, Cherubino, Figaro, whose arias, indeed, were composed on the text of the Venetian librettist, Lorenzo da Ponte.

Like sailors and ship's captains, the Venetians are fond of pets. They prefer cats to dogs, which are impractical in a city which has so little open space; most of the dogs one sees being led about on leashes have a touristic air and in fact they usually belong to foreigners, English or American. The signora has a cat, I discover, from hearing it claw at my windows, trying to get in. Its persistence tells me that it must live here, though the signora does not at first confess this. It is another displaced person, like the signore, and has been put out to live on the roof-tiles during the period when the apartment is rented. '*Permesso*,' says the signora, bursting into my sitting-room one morning with a paper full of garbage. She opens the window and thrusts the paper out. The cat eats, ravenously. '*Poverino*,' she cries, making a sad noise, while she glances apologetically in my direction. I do not understand why, if she pities the cat, she does not take it upstairs to live in her quarters; she has a terrace there. Perhaps the signore has objected. But I am determined not to take it as *my* lodger. The apartment is crowded with fragile china objects, which the signore values extortionately, as I have already learned on offering to pay for one that my coatsleeve had brushed off a table. Moreover, I am afraid of the cat, which pounds on the windows in a clawed frenzy, knowing that it belongs here and that I do not. It has become a perfect tiger, thanks to its life on the tiles.

In the kitchen reside two other candidates for the SPCA, if there only were one in Venice: a pair of pet goldfish in a blue-and white-china bowl. In the bottom of the bowl is a pile of five- and ten-lire pieces. That is all – no greenery, no algae, no scum. The water is clear and still. The fish are extremely pale, almost white, as though their colour had been bled from them, and very lethargic in their movements, not to say torpid. When I first looked at the apartment, I noted the fish and supposed they would go upstairs with the family. But when I moved in, they were still there in the kitchen, and the signora, drawing one of her most apologetic faces, as though she were about to ask me for a loan of one million lire, inquired whether they were in my way, whether I should mind if they stayed there. I did not mind, I said, but she must tell me what to feed them. Nothing, declared the signora, with a droll, sidelong look; she delights in mystifications. 'Non capisco,' I had to admit. 'Niente, niente!' airily repeated the signora. They did not have to be fed; that was the principle of this aquarium. The coins generated some sort of chemical in the water, and the fish lived on that; she had copied the idea from a fountain in Milan. I expressed doubt. Those poor blanched creatures were dying. Certainly not, scoffed the signora; she had had them nearly two years and they were in excellent health. As a proof of this, she plunged her long forefinger with its red-painted nail into the water and tickled one fish's tail; he feebly crept away from her touch. '*Ecco!*' she said, opening her pocketbook and tossing a fresh coin into the bowl. It was a bank too, she pointed out: if I needed change for my breakfast rolls, I had only to borrow from the fish. And there was nothing to clean; between the fish and the lire, the water stayed fresh. I nodded mutely, not being fluent enough in Italian to argue further.

Left to myself in the kitchen, I have tried feeding them bread crumbs. But they refuse this nourishment, rising languidly to inspect it and then turning their heads aside like peckish invalids; if they ingest a morsel, their flaccid jaws wanly seeking a purchase on it, they at once sink, inert, to the bottom, where they lie, spent, on their silvery bed of coins. Doubtless, they are accustomed to their diet, which keeps them in a state of bare animation, between life and death. The signora does not like it if she comes down and finds the water floury from the dissolving crumbs. I watch meekly while she dumps it out and pours in fresh water; the only excuse I can give for putting her to this trouble is that the fish look so very pale. ' "*Pallidi*," "*pallidi*," ' she scolds, between indignation and amusement. '*Non sono pallidi.*'

She laughs at the idea, which she finds typical of a

foreigner, that a fish can turn white from hunger. And though she does not understand English or French, she knows very well that the fish are being criticized when she hears exclamations proceeding from the kitchen if I am entertaining friends. ' "*Pallidi*," "*smorti*" ' – we are all the same, she jests. What can I do? I am too cowardly to put the poor creatures out of their misery, which a square meal of fish food would almost certainly bring about. I do not wish to incur the signora's wrath; in her brusque way, she has an affection for these fish that is based on their prodigious powers of survival. So I conclude that I had best leave them as they are and take them as an allegory on Venice, a society which lived in a bowl and drew its sustenance from the filth of lucre. Once flame-coloured, today it is a little pale and moribund, like the fish after two years of the signora's regimen.

A commercial people who lived solely for gain. Ruskin tried to show that this started with the 'degenerate' Venetians of the Renaissance, who sold their birthright for a mess of architectural pottage. He pictured Gothic Venice as a holy city flowering in its churches and its convents, in its religious processions and ceremonies – a sacred garden tended by humble artisans, supervised by upright doges and defended by brave captains. There was no division in this mystic city; all classes worked together, oblivious of self, in the radiance of a unifying belief. A 'noble,' 'manly' vision – the favourite adjectives of poor Ruskin, who was impotent, as his child-bride disclosed, seeking a decree of nullity after six years of 'white' marriage. Poor Ruskin, with his slide-rule and his ladder, a worshipper of the pragmatic fact, who was always flying in the face of the facts of life and of recorded history, for the sake of a vision. At the very period which he sought to hold up as a model for later ages – the period of the Crusades – Venetian rapacity was the scandal of the Christian world, and within Venice itself, the oligarchy strove with the popular faction; outside the convent of San Zaccaria, a doge was murdered in the street. The capture of St Mark's body from the heathens in Alexandria by two Venetian merchants in 828 – a favourite subject of Venetian painting – was almost the last action of Venetian merchants that could be considered 'holy.' In the first crusade, in the year 1100, the Venetians stopped off on the way to Jaffa to steal the body of St Nicholas, patron of sailors, from a monastery. In 1125, they stole the body of St Isidore from Christian Chios. From Tyre, in 1123, so many sacred relics were looted that they piled up on the Riva degli Schiavoni where the returning ships dumped them; the little tabernacles on the street corners date from Tyre's capture, a 'holy' enterprise that was undertaken for King Baldwin II of Jerusalem, in return for freedom from tolls throughout his kingdom, a quarter in Jerusalem, baths and ovens in Acre, and one-third of Tyre and its suburbs.

The granite pillars on the Molo came from Syria with the Doge Domenico Michiel, and St Mark's bronze lion was probably originally a chimera, Assyrian, under which the cunning Venetians slipped the Good Book. St Theodore, on the other column, started out, it is thought, as a Roman portrait-statue, and the crocodile (or whatever it is) consists of fifty assorted pieces rudely clamped together (Ruskin's 'organic unity').

Booty and trade concessions were extorted by the Venetians impartially from Christian and heathen. This impartiality, in the end, was what caused them to be hated, as sometimes the Jews have been, for being 'outside' the compact. As early as the great doge, Pietro Orseolo II, at the end of the tenth century, the Venetians had a trading agreement with the Saracens. They had concessions in Tyre, in Sidon, in Jaffa, in all the possessions of the fading Byzantine Empire, Rhodes and Cyprus, Chios and Candia, as well as in Constantinople itself, where 200,000 Venetians are supposed to have been living, in their separate quarter, in 1167, incurring so much odium that in 1171 all the Venetians in the Empire were arrested and their property was confiscated.

The Crusades were a bonanza for Venice, which acted as a shipping agent for Crusaders and treated the whole affair as a busines operation. They helped out with their, own troops at Jaffa and Tyre (after stipulating their price), but they did not 'take the Cross,' even in pretence, until the Fourth Crusade. Villehardouin, the chronicler of the Fourth Crusade, describes a moving scene in the Piazza, in which the doge and all his counsellors pledge themselves 'crying with one voice,' to come to the succour of the Holy Land, which was in the grip of Saladin. The French

chronicler sounds startled as he relates it; the Venetians had
never acted like this. But the chivalric scene, ending in a
glorious mass at St Mark's, had its sequel in a business
contract. Venice undertook to equip and transport an
army of 4,500 horses, 9,000 squires, 4,500 knights, and
20,000 foot soldiers and to keep them for one year in
provisions, in return for 85,000 silver marks payable in
four instalments. When the Crusaders did not pay up, the
Venetians drove a fresh bargain, by which the crusading
army would first undertake the capture of Zara, a Venetian port that had risen against its masters, and then proceed
to the rescue of Jerusalem. The pope's legate agreed, and
another stirring scene followed. The embarkation was a
sight to behold, the doge's galley, painted purple (a new
dye from the East), at the head of the great fleet, with a
band of musicians at the prow blowing on silver trumpets,
while the doge himself (ninety-five years old and blind,
some say; in his eighties and weak of sight, say others) sat
on his throne under a scarlet canopy, dressed in his cloak
of gold brocade, his son, the High Admiral, at his side.
The three hundred ships raised their banners aloft as the
priests chanted *Veni, Creator Spiritus*.

After this nautical pageant came business. The fleet
took Trieste and Muggia, for good measure, laid siege to
Zara, captured it, sacked it, and left it practically destroyed,
as though it were a Mohammedan town. The army
wintered in Zara and was persuaded by the old doge (or,
as some think, by the Hohenstaufens, whose willing tool he
was, through cupidity) to divert its aim from Jerusalem to

Christian Byzantium, with which the Venetians had been having some new commercial difficulties and which offered better prospects of pillage. The pope threatened excommunication, but he was unheeded. Byzantium was taken, a puppet emperor was installed, was overthrown, and eventually the Crusaders made themselves masters of the Empire and divided it up, the Venetians getting the famous 'quarter and a half-quarter' – the Cyclades and the Sporades, as well as many coastal cities in Epirus, on the Adriatic Gulf, and along the Albanian shore; they bought Crete from the marquis of Montferrat, who had no use for it himself.

This was the beginning of the Venezia Dominante and the end of the Eastern Empire. Under a series of Frankish counts, a Latin Empire was set up, with the Graustarkian name of Romania. The Greeks, under Michael Palaeologus, in time regained Constantinople and drove out the last of these 'Emperors.' But the Fourth Crusade had been fatal for Christendom, and the weakened, dismembered Empire fell prey to the Turks. The fall of Constantinople marked the end of Venetian involvement in the holy work of the Crusades. Having got what they wanted – their 'quarter and a half-quarter,' plus Crete – St Mark's merchants withdrew to the sidelines. In 1268, they signed a contract with St Louis for transport only on the eighth crusade. During the same century, the Emperor Baldwin II pawned his Crown of Thorns to the Venetian Morosini family for a loan of seven thousand ducats; in fact, he pawned it twice. Later, he pawned his son Philip to a

Cappello of Venice. The boy was redeemed by St Louis. Toward the end of the century, Venice lay under the pope's interdict and was also punished (it was thought) by Heaven with earthquakes and floods for having made an anti-crusade treaty with one of the Palaeologues. Not long after, unregenerate, the Venetians signed a treaty with the Turks and began trading in 'goods forbidden to Christians' – i.e., slaves, arms, and wood for shipbuilding; this was the equivalent of selling war material behind the Iron Curtain today. During this period, the only serious fighting the Venetians did in the Holy Land was with the Genoese, their rival traders. Trophies of their victory at Acre stand on the Piazzetta side of St Mark's: the Pietra del Bando, a short reddish column from which the Laws of the Republic were proclaimed, and the two strangely decorated pillars, Syrian art of the fifth or sixth century, carried off from the church of San Saba.

But it was the great Sack of Constantinople, in 1204, under the blind doge, that had netted the richest booty: the four little porphyry Moors (thought to be really four Roman Emperors who ruled jointly); the Horses (which had stood on high pedestals in the Hippodrome, a fact which saved their lives when the Crusaders set the town on fire); St Mark's wonder-working ikon, the Madonna Nicopeia, said to have been painted by St Luke; the top section (probably) of the Pala d'Oro, St Mark's great altarpiece in gold and jewels and enamels, which tourists today, having paid a fee, stand in line bug-eyed to examine. This top section was rifled, it is thought, from the Church of the Pantocrator. From Constantinople, certainly, came one of the bottom panels in which the Virgin is shown between the Empress Irene and the Emperor John Comnenus II, who has turned into the Doge Ordelaffo Falier. Such agile transformations were easy for the resourceful Venetians – the chimera into the winged lion, the emperor into the saint. The Emperor Justinian the Noseless, on St Mark's façade, a Syrian portrait of the eighth century, is called by the Venetians Count Carmagnola, after the general they decapitated nearby, on the Piazzetta. In the same way, by a characteristic turnabout the four little stolen Emperors have been converted by popular tradition into four Saracens who were turned to stone while trying to rob St Mark's treasury, outside which they stand embracing.

From the outside, as is often observed, St Mark's looks like an Oriental pavilion – half pleasure-house, half war-tent, belonging to some great satrap. Inside, glittering with jewels and gold, faced with precious Eastern marbles, jasper and alabaster, porphyry and verd-antique, sustained by Byzantine columns in the same materials, of varying sizes and epochs, scarcely a pair alike, this dark cruciform cave has the look of a robber's den. In the chapel of the Crucifix, with a pyramidal marble roof topped by a huge piece of Oriental agate and supported by six Byzantine columns in black and white African marble, stands a painted crucifix, of special holiness, taken from Constantinople. In the atrium, flanking St Clement's door, are two pairs of black and white marble columns, with wonderful lion's and eagle's heads in yellowish ivory; tradition says they came from the Temple of Solomon in Jerusalem. From Tyre came the huge block of Mount Tabor granite on the altar in the Baptistery – said to be the stone on which Christ was wont to pray. In the Zen chapel, the wall is lined with onion marbles and verd-antique, reputedly the gravestones of the Byzantine Emperors.

In the chapel of St Isidore sleeps the saint stolen from Chios; he was hidden for two centuries for fear of confiscation. St Theodore, stolen from Byzantium, was moved to San Salvatore. St Mark himself was lost for a considerable period, after a fire in 976, which destroyed most of the early church; he revealed his presence by thrusting forth his arm. He was not the original saint of Venice, but, so to speak, a usurper, displacing St Theodore. Thus, he himself, the patron, was a kind of thieving cuckoo bird, and his church, which was only the doge's private chapel, imitated him by usurping the functions of San Pietro in Castello, the seat of the Patriarch and the real Cathedral (until very recent times) of Venice. In the same style, the early doges had themselves buried, in St Mark's porch, in sarcophagi that did not belong to them, displacing the bones of old pagans and paleo-Christians.

Venice, unlike Rome or Ravenna or nearby Verona, had nothing of its own to start with. Venice, as a city, was a foundling, floating upon the waters like Moses in his basket among the bulrushes. It was therefore obliged to be inventive, to steal and improvise. Cleverness and adaptivity were imposed by the original situation, and the get-

up-and-go of the early Venetian business men was typical
of a self-made society. St Mark's Church is a (literally)
shining example of this spirit of initiative, this gift for
improvisation, for turning everything to account. It is
made of bricks, like most Venetian churches, since brick
was the easiest material to come by. Its external beauty
comes from the thin marble veneers with which the brick
surface is coated, just as though it were a piece of furniture.
These marbles for the most part, like the columns and
facing inside, were the spoils of war, and they were
put on almost haphazardly, green against grey, against
red or rose or white with red veining, without any
general principle of design beyond the immediate pleasure
of the eye. On the Piazzetta side, this gives the effect of
gay abstract painting. Parvenu art, more like painting
than architecture (as Herbert Spencer might say), and yet
it 'worked.' The marble veneers of St Mark's sides,
especially when washed by the rain so that they look like
oiled silk, are among the most beautiful things in Venice.
And it is their very thinness, the sense they give of being a
mere lustrous coating, a film, that makes them beautiful.
A palace of solid marble, rain washed, simply looks be-
draggled.

St Mark's as a whole, unless seen from a distance or at
twilight, is not beautiful. The modern mosaics (seventeenth century) are generally admitted to be extremely
ugly, and I myself do not care for some of the Gothic
statuary of the pinnacles. The horses, the coloured marble
veneers, the Byzantine Madonna of the front, the old

mosaic on the left, the marble columns of the portal, the gold encrustations of the top, the five grey domes with their strange ornaments, like children's jacks – these are the details that captivate. As for the rest, it is better not to look too closely, or the whole will begin to seem tawdry, a hodge-podge, as so many critics have said. The whole is not beautiful, and yet again it is. It depends on the light and the time of day or on whether you narrow your eyes, to make it look flat, a painted surface. And it can take you unawares, looking beautiful or horribly ugly, at a time you least expect. Venice, Henry James said, is as changeable as a nervous woman, and this is particularly true of St Mark's façade.

But why should it be beautiful at all? why should Venice, aside from its situation, be a place of enchantment? One appears to be confronted with a paradox. A commercial people who lived solely for gain – how could they create a city of fantasy, lovely as a dream or a fairy-tale? This is the central puzzle of Venice, the stumbling-block that one keeps coming up against if one tries to *think* about her history, to put facts of her history together with the visual fact that is there before one's eyes. It cannot be that Venice is a happy accident or a trick of light. I have thought about this a long time, but now it occurs to me that, as with most puzzles, the clue to the answer lies in the way the question is framed. 'Lovely as a dream or a fairy tale . . .' There is no contradiction, once you stop to think what images of beauty arise from fairy tales. They are images of money. Gold, caskets of gold, caskets of silver, the miller's

daughter spinning gold all night long, thanks to Rumpel-
stiltskin, the cave of Ali Baba stored with stolen gold and
silver, the underground garden in which Aladdin found
jewels growing on trees, so that he could gather them in
his hands, rubies and diamonds and emeralds, the Queen's
lovely daughter whose hair is black as ebony and lips are
red as rubies, treasure buried in the forest, treasure guarded
by dogs with eyes as big as carbuncles, treasure guarded by
a Beast – this is the spirit of the enchantment under which
Venice lies, pearly and roseate, like the Sleeping Beauty,
changeless throughout the centuries, arrested, while the
concrete forest of the modern world grows up around her.

A wholly materialist city is nothing but a dream incar-
nate. Venice is the world's unconscious: a miser's glittering hoard, guarded by a Beast whose eyes are made of
white agate, and by a saint who is really a prince who has
just slain a dragon.

A list of goods in which the early Venetian merchants
trafficked arouses a sense of pure wonder: wine and grain
from Apulia, gems and drugs from Asia, metal-work,
silk, and cloth of gold from Byzantium and Greece. These
are the gifts of the Magi, in the words of the English hymn
'Pearls from the ocean and gems from the mountain;
myrrh from the forest and gold from the mine.' During
the Middle Ages, as a part of his rightful revenue, the doge
had his share in the apples of Lombardy and the crayfish
and cherries of Treviso – the Venetian mind, interested
only in the immediate and the solid, leaves behind it for
our minds, clear, dawn-fresh images out of fairy tales.

3

A Pound of Flesh

Shylock, of course, was not the Merchant of Venice. The Merchant was the hero, Antonio. Shylock was only a moneylender. But popular belief declines to make the distinction and persists in thinking that Shylock was the merchant, i.e., that Venetian merchants were all Shylocks. This reflects the reputation borne by the Venetians in the outside world. They had a name for sharp dealing, for 'sticking together,' artful diplomacy, business 'push,' and godless secularism – traits familiarly ascribed to the Jews. Anti-Semitism is often traced to a medieval hatred of capitalism. To the medieval mind, the Jew was the capitalist par excellence. But this could also be said of the Venetian, whose palace was his emporium and his warehouse. Certainly the hatred excited by Venice during the late Middle Ages and early Renaissance, the wave of revulsion that swept over Europe, culminating in the League of Cambrai of 1508, had an irrational, supercharged quality that was like modern anti-Semitism.

The Venetians were more feared than they deserved to be. Boundless ambition was attributed to them; they were accused of seeking world-domination, which seems to have been far from their thoughts. Even Machiavelli was taken in by this myth, and the language of the pact of Cambrai, signed by most of the great powers of the Christian world, anticipates the Protocols of the Elders of Zion – a case of mass hysteria being manipulated by a political adventurer, who, in this instance, was the Emperor Maximilian. Early in 1509, abetted by the pope, this German prince issued a manifesto, in which he cited the Venetians as 'conspiring the ruin of everyone,' and he called on all peoples to partake in a just vengeance, to put out 'like a common fire, the insatiable cupidity of the Venetians and their thirst for domination.' It was Maximilian himself, as a matter of fact, 'the last of the knights,' as he was styled, who was plotting a universal kingdom, and who, shortly afterwards, had the notion of making himself Pope. But Christendom agreed with him that Venice was the real enemy. He was joined by the King of France, the King of Spain, the King of Hungary, the Duke of Milan, and the Duke of Savoy. The Pope, Julius II (friend of Raphael, Michelangelo, and Bramante), laid Venice under an interdict and proclaimed the war against her to be a holy crusade, in which all measures were justified. The results were not as conclusive as might have been expected; the allies fell out among themselves, and Venice was only partly dismembered. Nevertheless, this holy war against her was a moral shock from which Venice did not recover. Her decline as a power dates from the Cambrai period. To be disliked on such a scale and with so little provocation is unsettling to a nation which is, above all, rational in its approach to politics.

There were those who saw it coming. In 1423, the old doge, Tommaso Mocenigo, called the chief magistrates to his deathbed to warn them against territorial expansion and the suspicions it would be bound to arouse. He argued in terms of the balance-sheet: six million ducats a year in exports, with an annual return of two million; three thousand ships of two hundred tons, manned by seventeen thousand sailors; three hundred shipping firms with a pay-roll of eight thousand hands; forty-five galleys with eleven thousand sailors, three thousand shipwrights and three thousand caulkers; three thousand silk weavers, sixteen thousand fustian weavers . . . This investment could only be safeguarded by a peaceful policy. The other way lay universal odium, war abroad, bankruptcy at home. If 'the young procurator,' Francesco Foscari (48 years old), were elected doge, 'the man who has ten thousand ducats will have a thousand; the man who has two houses will have have one; you will spend your silver and gold, reputation and honour. Instead of being master in your city, you will be at the mercy of your troops, your military men and captains.'

The young procurator *was* elected, and the old doge's prophecy came true. Foscari's *terra ferma* adventures greatly increased Venice's holdings on the peninsula, but they left her much poorer and, as Mocenigo had said, dependent on her military men, soldiers of fortune, like General Carmagnola, who, having been paid for his prowess, preferred taking the baths at Lucca to fighting for the Republic. Yet even under 'the young procurator,'

Venetian foreign policy lacked élan and firmness. It shuffled about, undecided, the merchants of the Senate being always of two minds as to whether these land wars would really be good for business in the long run, as the war party claimed. At the slightest reverse, querulous voices began demanding peace. In all the confused wars of Francesco Foscari, the only military action that was done with resolution and dispatch was the arrest of General Carmagnola – once it was agreed upon. He was apprehended in the Doge's Palace and politely shown the way to prison, before he or anyone outside was aware of the Republic's suspicions of him. Under torture, he confessed. He was tried for treason and decapitated. And it was all done so swiftly and succinctly that it is even possible that the unfortunate mercenary was innocent. The rest of Europe gaped; that was not the way *condottieri* were treated. But such summary decisions, on the domestic scene, were what the Venetians were good at.

In the early days, under a Byzantine influence, they were fond of blinding their doges, over a brazier of live coals. Four doges met this punishment in the eighth and ninth centuries. Later, a refinement was introduced; the erring doge was seized by his people, who shaved his beard and compelled him to retire to a monastery or else banished him to Constantinople. This happened on three occasions. Other doges fled secretly to monasteries to avoid being murdered by their subjects; one of these, Pietro Orseolo I, lived twenty-nine years of pious life after his escape and was eventually canonized. By 1172, out of fifty doges, nineteen had been slain, banished, mutilated or deposed. The convent of San Zaccaria, not far from San Marco, proved to be a fatal spot for several wearers of the ducal bonnet, which, as a matter of fact, was a present from the nuns to one of the doges. Pietro Tradonico was slain as he was leaving vespers there in 864. Tribuno Memmo was forcibly retired there in 992. After Tradonico's murder, a new and safer (as it was hoped) entrance was made to the convent, on the other side, from SS. Filippo and Giacomo. But events did not prove it to be so. The doge Vitale Michiel II was struck down in 1172, just outside the gate, as he was hurrying to sanctuary.

The young procurator himself, when he reached old age, was deposed in summary fashion for sympathizing with his son, whom the Venetians had condemned unjustly. After his deposition, he sent a touching message to an old noble who was his friend, a message that evokes the banished kings of Shakespeare. 'My dear good friend,' he said to Memmo's son, Jacopo, 'tell him [your father] to come and see me. We will go and amuse ourselves in a boat, rowing to the monasteries.'

The Venetians were not sentimental; they were efficient. The past did not count for them until it had been gilded in ritual. They threw their greatest captain, Vettor Pisani, into jail because of a single naval defeat that was, in fact, their own fault. When Sansovino's ceiling in the Old Library fell, they clapped him at once into jail, unmindful of the beauties he had contributed to Venetian architecture. The famous mysteries of Venetian history, the plot of

Marino Falier, the Spanish conspiracy, are mysterious because the Republic acted so promptly that nobody knew what had happened, and the public was left to guess. In 1618, in May, two bodies appeared on the Piazzetta one morning, hanging by one leg between gibbets. Sir Henry Wotton, the English poet and ambassador to the Republic from James I, wrote to Buckingham of seeing the two bodies hanging between 'the two fatal pillars' in St Mark's place. A day or so later, a third body appeared. They hung there – silent warnings – all through the festivities following the doge's election and through the Wedding of the Adriatic on Ascension Day. Who they were or what they had done, nobody was told; rumour declared that a conspiracy had been suppressed. A Spanish conspiracy, some said; more likely a French conspiracy, others decided. The bodies were three Frenchmen. This is all that is known for certain about the famous Spanish Conspiracy, the subject of Otway's *Venice Preserved*.

In the absence of facts, poetry and rumour surround Venetian events. Marino Falier, a member of the highest aristocracy, described by Petrarch as a man noted for his wisdom, who was elected doge without having sought the office, suddenly after eight months of power, in the seventy-seventh year of his life, conspired to overthrow the Republic and make himself prince with the help of the arsenal workers and other disaffected plebeians and middle-class persons, including a man named Calendario, the architect of the Doge's Palace. Falier confessed to the crime, but his motives remain unknown, as blank as the black space in the Hall of the Great Council where his portrait once hung in the long row of doges. According to one legend, a young noble had insulted his wife; the old man, hot-tempered, took offence and turned against his own class. Popular opinion ascribed the whole affair to a fog or mist that sprang up, inexplicably, in the harbour as he was arriving in the Bucintoro to take office, so that he ran aground at San Giorgio in Alega. '*Sinistro pede palatium ingressus*,' Petrarch wrote. Thanks to the fog, he entered the palace on the left foot, so to speak, passing between the two columns on the Molo where executions were held instead of going the usual way, over the Bridge of Straw. In any case, eight months later he was beheaded; his body was placed in a common barge from the *traghetto* – the sort of barge used in the Great Plague (1348) of the same period, with boatmen crying out, 'Any dead bodies?' and carting them off like garbage to the outlying cemeteries. Falier, symbolically pestilential, was allowed four torches, a single priest and an acolyte to see him to the family vault in SS. Giovanni and Paolo. Byron made a play of him.

The architect, Calendario, was strangled for his part in the conspiracy and strung up between the two red columns on the Doge's Palace loggia, on the side facing the Piazzetta. They are supposed to have turned red from the blood that ran down them, on this and other occasions. And here, by the way, is another case of twinning. There are *two* sets of 'fatal pillars,' the big granite ones on the Molo and the smaller, red ones of the Doge's Palace loggia.

Both were used for public executions and for the display of corpses, and it is hard to tell, in any given account, which ones are meant. Wotton wrote Buckingham that the more general practice was for the executioner to drown his victims quietly in the Canal degli Orfani, 'one of their deepest channels.' This 'Orphans' Canal,' curiously enough, is not shown to tourists today, which is surprising, since Venice cultivates the *ricordi* of her blackest acts, such as the 'column of infamy' put up to Bajamonte Tiepolo, another aristocratic conspirator, on the site of his house in the Campo Sant' Agostino. In the eighteenth century, the column was taken by a rich patrician as an ornament for his villa near Padua, but a little plaque in the pavement commemorates the spot. Bajamonte, young, handsome, and rich, was the most attractive of all Venice's rebels. A gay little jingle in Venetian dialect tells the story of 'the great cavalier' who crossed the Rialto Bridge and came marching up the Merceria with his standards flying, only to find that the people's temper had turned against him:

> '*Del mille trecento e diese*
> *A mezzo el mese delle ceriese*
> *Bagiamonte passo el ponte*
> *E per esso fo fatto el consegio di diese.*'

> 'In one thousand three hundred and ten
> In the middle of the month of cherries
> Bajamonte crossed the Bridge

And for that they made the Council of Ten.'

His standard-bearer, with a flag inscribed, 'Liberty,' was killed by a brick thrown by a woman of the people from her balcony – a disconcerting omen for a popular uprising. Just past the Clock Tower, the sottoportico del Cappello Nero has a relief known as 'The Old Woman with the Brick.' Below, on the street, a little white stone purports to indicate the precise spot where the brick fell.

The *ricordi* or souvenirs of today are yesterday's reminders or warnings. And this, again, is suggestive of a politics of old men, a counting-house politics that constantly reminds its citizens, as if in a series of mottoes, that honesty is the best policy. Those bodies hanging on the Molo (or from the Doge's Palace), that column of infamy, that vacant space on the wall where a doge has been erased – these are not barbaric shows of vengeance but daily reminders, such as might be hung over the desks of clerks in a big old-fashioned office. Venetian history (as opposed to Venetian pageantry) is singularly lacking in colour. A doge is deposed, after many years of service to the state, in the same dry style that an employee is given his dismissal. 'You had better quit,' the Ten warn old Foscari. 'I won't quit; you'll have to fire me,' replies the failing doge. The individual is expected to set the firm's interest first, and the individual scarcely figures in the firm's records, unless a black mark has been set against his name. Horatio Brown comments on the scarcity of biographical material on Venice's great men; it is hard, he indicates, to write the history of a state in which nothing personal is known about its soldiers and statesmen. The Republic took every safeguard against popular intrusions, on the one hand, and against manifestations of individuality in the aristocracy, on the other. Its leaders are all subordinates, and its sole heroine, the poor Queen of Cyprus, Caterina Cornaro, meekly handing her Crown over to the Republic, achieved her place in history by an act of renunciation. Wotton says they chose on purpose doges who were not likely to live long, and he describes a candidate counterfeiting feebleness in the hope of getting elected.

The Venetian state was a closed concern. After 1287, nobody could hold office who was not inscribed in the Golden Book – the ancient rolls of the nobility, which were finally burned, in Napoleon's time, at the foot of the Tree of Liberty. The machinery for electing a doge in its perfected form was like an elaborate burglar-alarm system; nobody unauthorized could get in, and it responded to the slightest jar in the atmosphere. Out of the Great Council (consisting at first of 480, then of 600, and finally of 1200 nobles), 9 were picked by lot to elect 40 electors, who had to be chosen by a majority of at least seven. The 40 drew lots to see which 12 would elect 25 more by a majority of at least seven. These 25 then drew lots to see which 9 would elect 45 by a majority of at least seven. Finally, these 45 drew lots to choose 11, who would vote for 41 electors, who would elect the doge by a majority of at least 25.

According to Wotton, the method of choosing the doge
was supposed to have been invented by a Benedictine, and
'the whole mysterious frame therein doth much savour
of the cloister.' The doge lived a cloistered existence in the
exquisite prison of the ducal palace. He had to swear a
ducal oath on taking office, and this oath, which kept getting longer and longer and longer, was simply a list of
things he promised not to do. He could not own property
outside the Republic. Neither he nor his sons could marry
a foreigner without the Great Council's permission. He
was forbidden to display his coat-of-arms. No member of
his family was allowed to hold a political post. He was
hedged about by the Forty, by the Signory of six ducal
councillors, by the Senate, by the sixteen Grand Sages, by
the Ten, and (after Cambrai) by the Three Inquisitors, who
served for one year only and had the whole charge of
public safety and private morals within their control.
After the doge's death, a wax figure, his simulacrum, was
laid out in the chamber of Piovego, on the first floor of the
ducal palace, and a scrutiny was made of all his acts in
office. This symbolic dummy, clad in the ducal robes and
wearing the bonnet, was not very different from the
living man, who was carried about in a chair in processions
like a holy image or relic.

The doge was not the only prisoner of the system. It
was a trap in which every noble Venetian was caught on
attaining his majority. At the age of twenty-five, a young
aristocrat was introduced into the maze of duties and
ceremonies – at once decorative and confining like the

eighteenth-century maze of the Pisani on the grounds of their villa at Stra. A member of the Great Council (i.e., any member of the nobility) was forbidden to associate with foreigners. Wotton, one morning, found Antonio Foscarini, the former ambassador to England, hanging by one leg from a gibbet in the Square; his association with Lady Arundel, an Englishwoman, had lent credence to an accusation of treason, though in fact he was only in love with her. The three Capi of the Ten – the most powerful members of the bureaucracy before the Inquisitors superseded them – were required to live strictly apart from the rest of the community, staying at home and associating with no one during their term of office, which was limited to one month. Dress was prescribed for the nobility, though some of its members were very impoverished; beggars dressed in silk – the compulsory material for nobles – were a common sight in Venice. The Inquisitors themselves were subject to a fear peculiar to their function: the fear of reprisals for acts they had committed during their year of power. Wotton tells of a Leonardo Mocenigo, who was appointed Captain of the Sea and who refused the post because he regarded the appointment as a trap set for him by the enemies he had made when he was Inquisitor of State. But escape was not open to such a man; he could not be permitted to vanish into private life. He was punished by the Ten for refusing.

Long before Casanova, the terror struck by the Inquisitors reached a pitch of melodrama. Yet they were not as effective as their legend. Their decrees, especially in the field of private morals and of dress, were openly disregarded, and the foreign embassies were havens of thugs and ruffians who defied any control. In this atmosphere of private violence, the Inquisitors sometimes appeared positively benign, like Platonic Guardians. And unlike the modern police state, to which it is often compared, Venice feared power and surrounded it with checks and deterrents. Its real desire was for business as usual. Its foreign policy, even in its expansionist phase, always had a protectionist aim: the safeguarding of markets. Narrow, short-sighted men, narrow, blinkered policies – its enemies flattered the Republic when they imputed a thirst for dominion to it. Wherever the Republic conquered territory, it tended to revert to the habits it had formed in the near East in the eleventh and twelfth centuries. Old Dandolo refused the crown after the capture of Constantinople. He was content, as his forbears had been, to let others rule. He stipulated his 'quarter and a half-quarter' of the Roman Empire as his forbears had stipulated a Venetian 'quarter,' with baths and ovens, for the Venetian merchants. A modified self-rule was offered by Venice to her subject-lands; Venice could not tax herself with the heavy apparatus of Empire. The result of this moderate policy was that she regained many of the Italian lands she had lost during the wars of the League of Cambrai. Treviso, Verona, Padua, Vicenza – they came back to her, voluntarily, after a real taste of the oppressor's boot.

Venice was never feudal, and it never acquired feudal habits of mind. Because of its impregnable situation, moated by lagoons, it did not require walls or fortified castles or brawling bands of men-at-arms. Its noblemen bore no titles, only the designation, 'N. H.,' for nobleman. The present-day counts are creations of the Austrians. It had a citizen army in its days of valour and was the last of the Italian states to begin hiring mercenary captains. The citizen, in his domestic aspect, tranquil in the enjoyment of his goods, was in fact a Venetian ideal. Reasonable, peaceful, avid only for consumption, unsuperstitious, it was a country, said Wotton, 'in general not much inclined to presagement but rather every man busy about himself.' The purpose of the intricate state machinery was to create, precisely, a *machine* for government, in which the wills and passions of men would have no part; the Venetian government was an invention in the field of political science, a patented device, not unlike the signora's goldfish bowl, in which all the components are supposed to cancel each other out, achieving a perfect equipoise. If the machine became a Frankenstein's monster, that was a paradoxical result of the original intention. The attempt to evolve a perfect product of any kind tends, by some law of limit, to conjure up its contrary: the demand for perfect love, for example, elicits perfect hate.

The Venetians, as I have said, were hated in much the same fashion as the Jews, for being outside the compact. They were hated and envied and they knew it. They were a people apart; like the Jews, the children of an Exodus. Their remarkable survival gave them a certain sense of chosenness. They regarded themselves as the true heirs of

Rome, and this was right to a degree. The Venetian Republic was the only state to emerge intact from the ruins of the Roman Empire. They were governed originally, on the islets, by tribunes. Their patrician democracy corresponded to that of the Roman Republic; their military men and admirals, summoned from private life to lead in a time of peril, had a good deal of Cincinnatus about them. The fear of kingship (which amounted almost to phobia) was Roman; so, on the other hand, was their sexual vice and their delicate voluptuous luxury, which makes one think, often, of Pompeii. Their practicality, too, and their money-greed recall the Roman capitalists, Crassus the Triumvir of the late Republic.

The legacy of Rome is evident, but Roman grossness is lacking, the grossness of the Empire and its swollen, mad, deified Emperors. The Venetians seem to have had the later Rome always before their eyes, as a terrible object-lesson. That was why they circumscribed their doges and kept down their military captains; they feared a Caesar for ten obsessive centuries. '*Morte ai tiranni*,' the old woman is supposed to have screeched as she threw her brick at Bajamonte. It is as heirs, chiefly, of the antique Republic that the Venetians present themselves, a chosen strain, perpetuated, in a city that is like the Heavenly Jerusalem: 'Flash the streets with jasper, Shine the gates with gold, Flows the gladdening river, Shedding joys untold.'

No doubt, they did not compare themselves with that other chosen people whom they permitted to live in their midst, but a subtle relationship existed, nonetheless. The

Venetian Jew enjoyed a favoured status in the medieval period. He was allowed to set up loan banks, 'for the relief of the Venetian poor.' to trade with the East, to practise medicine, and to sell old clothes – concessions that do not seem very great today but which reflected a high degree of tolerance on the part of the Republic. Resident Jews were obliged to wear the yellow hat (later a red hat), but exceptional Jews were often exempted from the rule. Most remarkable of all, the authorities would not permit the Jews to be persecuted. During the wave of anti-Semitic feeling that ran through Italy in 1475, the doge ordered protection for the Jews and prohibited inflammatory sermons. This was only one of many edicts restraining the enthusiasm of the friars who came to Venice, preaching death to the Jews. There were two bad episodes. Some Jews from near Treviso were burned to death by the Republic for the alleged ritual murder of a child in 1480, and the whole community was expelled from Vicenza, on the same suspicion, in 1485. But these, at any rate, were official acts. What the Republic refused to concede its citizens was the right to do arbitrary violence to Jewish persons and property – a right that appeared virtually innate to the rest of the Christian world. That, on the contrary, a Jew had rights, was the essence of Venetian law, whose spirit is summed up, correctly, by Shakespeare's merchant, Antonio.

> 'The duke cannot deny the course of law;
> For the commodity that strangers have

With us in Venice if it be denied,
Will much impeach the justice of this state;
Since that the trade and profit of this city
Consisteth of all nations.'

'The trade and profit of this city' – here the Venetian
cash-register rings, for if the Republic tolerated the Jews,
it did so for a price. No Jew, including a native, could stay
in Venice without a permit, which cost a considerable
sum of money, and which had to be renewed every five,
seven, or ten years for an additional fee. From time to time,
the Republic would contemplate the expulsion of the
Jews but it would change its mind, expediently, after
negotiations with the chief Jews of the city during which a
bargain would be struck, a rather one-sided bargain, for the
Jews had no recourse, generally, but to pay the price set by
the Republic for its continued toleration. The notion that a
Jew had rights did not imply any doctrine of equality; the
Jews had *specific* rights, the rights he paid to enjoy.

The Venetians were tolerant, but the Ghetto was a
Venetian invention, a typical piece of Venetian machinery,
designed to 'contain' the Jews while profiting from them,
just as the doge was 'contained.' The word comes from the
Venetian word, foundry, and the New Ghetto, into which
the Jews were directed, the day after Pentecost, 1516, was
the New Foundry, where cannons had formerly been cast.
The idea was devised to meet the problem of the Jewish
refugees who were fleeing into the city from the mainland
towns during the wars of the League of Cambrai. Venetian

geography made segregation easy. The area of the New
Foundry was an island, on which the Jews were shut up
every day at nightfall. The three gates were closed and
locked; Christian guards, paid by the Jews, were posted,
at first in boats on the canal. The house windows facing
outwards were blocked up, by decree, so that the Ghetto
turned a blind face to the city. In the morning, when the
Marangona rang, the gates were unlocked. The New
Ghetto was made for German and Italian Jews; later, the
Old Foundry or Old Ghetto was added, for the Levan-
tines. When crowding became a problem, tall houses
resembling skyscrapers were built, which still can be seen
in the main square of the Ghetto Nuovo – a strange,
picturesque sight, as if a modern slum were expressed in
an ancient idiom, like a prophecy.

The Venetians, needless to say, were alert to the picturesque aspect. The Ghetto became a tourist haunt almost as
soon as it was devised. Thomas Coryat, an Englishman
who walked from Somerset to Venice, described his
peregrinations through the Ghetto in 1608. The Jews of
that time were prosperous and handsome, the women, he
said, 'as beautiful as I ever saw, . . . so gorgeous in their
apparel, jewels, chains of gold, and rings adorned with
precious stones, that some of our English countesses do
scarce exceed them, having marvailous long trains like
Princesses that are borne up by waiting women serving
for the same purpose.' He got into a theological dispute
with a rabbi and was worsted by him. In 1629, the Duke of
Orleans, brother of the King of France, visited the Ghetto

in state, with his train, and listened to a sermon in the Spanish synagogue. In 1635, this synagogue was restored and enlarged by Longhena.

I went there on Yom Kippur and stood in the women's gallery; below, under the dark, massive, carved ceiling, a few men and boys in American-style hats were intoning the service. The Ghetto today is one of the poorest sections of Venice, in the northern quarter, where a melancholy light embraces San Giobbe, image of patience, on the west, and the deserted Abbey of the Misericordia, image of mercy, on the east. It no longer draws many tourists or Venetians either; this is the only area where I have seen children beg. But in the eighteenth century, priests and patricians would come to hear a famous rabbi preach; Benedetto Marcello, the Venetian composer, visited it for inspiration for his Psalms. It was one of the great centres of rabbinical culture in Europe, while outside the Ghetto gates, during the sixteenth and seventeenth centuries, Christian Venice itself was the seat of Hebrew book-printing. The Venetian Jews, in their red hats, were called on to supply learning, lore, and luxurious appointments for the foreign world. Henry VIII enlisted the opinion of a Venetian rabbi in his divorce suit against Katharine of Aragon. Another Jewish prodigy, the gambling rabbi, Leone da Modena, was recruited by Henry Wotton to write an account of Jewish rites and ceremonies for the pedant-king, James I. The ambassador hired most of his furniture for his palace on the Grand Canal from a Jew named Luzzati, who also supplied him with pictures, halberds, bucklers and arms – the decorative accessories of the period. It was customary for visiting foreigners, renting palazzi, to resort to Jewish second-hand dealers for articles de luxe sold or pawned by the nobility: hangings and plate, Veroneses and Titians, even gondola-trappings.

But for all this the Venetians exacted a veritable pound of flesh. They bled the Jewish community in every conceivable way. Since the law forbade Jews to own land, the Republic forced them to *rent* the Ghetto in its entirety on a long lease; the day the Jews moved in, rentals were raised one-third. In the course of years, many Jews left Venice for Holland, because of Venetian rapacity; others died of the plague. But the community continued to pay rent on houses that stood unoccupied – that was the contract. They were gouged for taxes, for tribute, for the army, for the navy, for the upkeep of the canals; they were forced to keep open their loan banks and to pay the government for the privilege, long after these had ceased to be profitable. They were not permitted to go out of business, just as the doge was not permitted to refuse his office or to resign it. This relentless policy continued to the point where in 1735, the *Inquisitori sopra gli Ebrei* had to confess to the Senate that the Jews under their supervision were insolvent, and the community was declared bankrupt, by official state decree. There was no more to be got from them, the Venetians, as realists, conceded, crossing the account off their books with one of those resigned shrugs commonly thought of as Jewish.

When Napoleon opened the gates of the Ghetto in

1797, it was little but a collection of alms-houses, supported by the handful of prosperous Jews left. A Tree of Liberty was erected in the campo, and the priests from the neighbouring churches came in to dance the carmagnole and fraternize with the starveling survivors of Venetian toleration. The Jews were free to move now, but according to Venetian legend they did not have the strength to do so. Hence they are there still.

A sad story, not without its ironical aspects, a typical Jewish joke, in fact, resigned and wry. The Republic was bankrupt too, of course. It had lived like a grasshopper, while the burdened Jew had toiled like the ant – and they had both come out at the same place. The Venetian today has a sardonic character: the result, no doubt, of his fall from glory. He still feels himself to be chosen, however, chosen in a twofold sense, singled out on the one hand for special favours and, on the other, to be mocked by Fate. The Venetians, everyone says, are not like the other Italians. The Venetians are grave and dignified, full of ceremonious courtesy; at the same time, they are ironical and quick with a retort. They have become peaceful and passive – non-violent. There is very little crime in Venice. This pacific temper, this dryness, this ceremony – all shadowed with a certain faraway sadness – these graven traits of character suggest a 'Jewish' strain in the Venetian nature. The high-nosed, dark-eyed Venetian dignitaries painted by Titian and Tintoretto have the look of priests of the Temple; the Old Testament prophets in Venetian art are always completely convincing, as are the Biblical scenes of Jacopo Bassano, which are like sudden illuminations of the life of Canaan, where patriarchal chieftains, with their wives and sons and concubines, grazed their well-fed flocks. Set apart, much hated, the Venetian traders shared a strand of the Jewish destiny, which was interwoven with their own in a fabric commonly thought of as 'eastern.' The Jews were the last representatives of the Eastern bazaars to remain in Venice; when the Star of David set in the eighteenth-century ghetto, Venice herself was extinguished.

4

The Monk

Che vuol dire Calvinista? Siamo Cristiani quanto il Papa e cristiani moriremo a dispetto di chi non lo vorria.' 'Calvinist – what does that mean? We are just as good Christians as the Pope, and Christians we shall die, whether anybody else likes it nor not.' So – tartly – spoke Leonardo Donato, rebuffing the charge of heresy that had been put upon the Republic during the quarrel with the pope, Paul V. The Venetians always claimed to be as good Christians as the pope, if not a little better. Had they not, in 855, given Benedict III refuge with the nuns in San Zaccaria when he was hiding from the anti-pope, Anastasius? Had they not, in 1177, forced the Emperor Frederick Barbarossa to kiss the pope's foot in St Mark's atrium and hold the papal mule outside on the Piazza while the Holy Father mounted – an intervention that earned the doge the ring with which he wedded the Adriatic on Ascension Day, the ring that epitomized the new Venetian vainglory, for the doge, who previously had gone to the sea on that feast day to be cleansed of sins ('Purge me with hyssop and I shall be clean'), now came, with the pope's blessing, as a conquering bridegroom ('We wed thee, Sea, in token of true and perpetual dominion')? Indeed, when Donato spoke, the picture showing Redbeard kissing Alexander's foot had just been hung (1603) in the Hall of the Great Council, whose whole long north wall was devoted to works celebrating Frederick's humiliation and Venice's espousal of the pope's cause: 'The doge Sebastiano Ziani recognizing the pope, who was hiding in the Convent of the Carità,' 'The pope in St Mark's giving the doge the white wax taper as a symbol of ducal authority,' 'The pope blessing the doge's armada as it sailed out against Frederick,' 'The doge receiving from the pope a consecrated sword,' 'The doge receiving the ring,' 'The doge receiving the golden umbrella,' etc. – events largely imaginary but grandiosely painted by the sons and assistants and epigones of Tintoretto, Bassano, and Veronese.

Città apostolica e santa – with their hundred-odd churches, their ceremonies and processions, their religious guilds and confraternities and bird-choirs of nuns, the Venetians had won from the Holy See itself a designation that put the city on a par with Rome. They had fought the Turk for Christendom, while Christendom sat by. One of their captains, Marcantonio Bragadin, the brave defender of Cyprus, had been been mutilated by the infidel and then flayed alive on the public square of Famagosta; his skin was stuffed with straw and paraded through the streets under a red umbrella. This straw man, hoisted to a yard-arm, was then carried off to the Turkish Arsenal, where it stayed for nine years, till St Mark's enterprising sailors stole it and brought it back to San Gregorio.

This was Venetian piety, but the Catholic powers smiled
behind their hands at the spectacle of Venice worsted by
Mahomet. Shortly before Famagosta, du Bellay, nephew
of the cardinal, framed that mordant smile in a sonnet,
deriding the Sposalizio:

> '... *ces vieux coquz vont épouser la mer*
> *Dont ils sont les maris et le Turc l'adultère.*'

'These old cuckolds' had a just sense of grievance
against the Catholic powers who abandoned them in their
struggle against the Turkish enemy, so that only a bastard
prince, Don John of Austria, 'rising from a doubtful seat
and half-attainted stall,' came to help them in their great
victory at Lepanto, a victory which was never followed
up, owing to the treachery of Spain, which did not care
for the spectacle of a Venetian boat entering the Lido with
red Turkish flags (which can still be seen in the Museo
Correr) trailing from the stern and Turkish turbans piled
on the deck. 'Envying us, they hate us, and hating us, they
lay snares for us,' as Morosini said. Spain could not bear
that '*questa sola repubblica, questo sol angolo d'Italia,*' should
be free.

Who was more Christian – the Venetians demanded –
when the stakes were down, than they? They were insulted by the charge of heresy, as, indeed, heretics generally
are: Tito preened himself on being at least as good a
Communist as Stalin, and Luther had no doubt that he was
more orthodox than his adversaries.

The fact is, there was more truth in the Holy See's suspicions than the stiff-necked Donato, who soon became doge, admitted. In 1605, when he made his angry rejoinder, Venice was not Protestant – *not yet*, Sir Henry Wotton would have added. The English ambassador (though the Venetians denied it) was just what the pope said he was: a secret agent of Protestantism, working to wean the Republic away from the old faith. The Curia complained that Wotton was introducing dangerous books into Venice, and the doge retorted: ' . . . it is impossible for the Republic to search the boxes of the English ambassador, when we are absolutely certain that he is living most reserved and quietly, causing no scandal whatever. We know nothing of these dangerous works, and if they had existed we should have heard of them, for we do not keep our eyes shut in matters of religion.' But that was just what the doge was doing, as we know from Wotton's letters to his Protestant master, James I. The Republic knew very well that Wotton was busily importing Protestant Bibles – translated into Italian by the Calvinist Diodati – to circulate among the population; the embassy was bulging with anti-Catholic literature, including James' own *Basilikon Doron*, a fire-breathing work, which Wotton actually had the sangfroid to try to present to the doge.

Under the papal nuncio's scrutiny, the doge felt obliged to decline the gift, with private apologies to Wotton. But there was fertile soil here, Wotton was able to report to his master, fertile soil for proselytization, and for a new Protestant alliance in which the maritime Republic would join. Strange as this seems today, it was for a moment an historical possibility. In the Great Council, as another agent reported, there was a party of evangelical nobles, thirty of them avowed Protestants. There were 4,000 to 10,000 'of the religion' among the general population, including, however, many foreigners who were enjoying the toleration of the Republic. Marot, du Bellay's enemy, had been there, not long before, when he had been obliged to flee from France under a suspicion of heresy. Venice, in fact, was swarming not only with Protestants but with mere suspects, refugees from the Inquisition, as well as many atheists, Orthodox Greeks, and Jews. In the previous century, Lorenzo Lotto had executed, on commission, portraits of Luther and his wife – imaginary likenesses, since he had never seen them. A Venetian writer, Alvise Cornaro, declared that Venice had introduced three bad customs into Italy: first, adulation and ceremony; second, Lutheranism; and third, debauchery. More important, though, to Wotton's hopes than the presence of all sorts of dissenters, was the fact that many of the clergy themselves were disaffected, hostile to the Curia and the Jesuits, and ready to discuss, very freely, the possibility of a break with Rome. Among these thoughtful priests was one of the clearest minds of the age, Paolo Sarpi, the great Servite friar who became the Republic's chief counsellor during the contest with the Church, which finally came to a head in the excommunication and interdict of 1606.

Wotton was delighted with the interdict; and so was his Majesty in London. They did not doubt the power of the Republic to survive the pope's ban. The holy, apostolic city was used to living under interdict. The first happened in 1173, just four years before Barbarossa's visit, when the Venetians, under the same Doge Ziani, gave offence to the same pope, Alexander III, by demolishing the old church of San Geminiano without permission, while they were making some improvements in St Mark's Square. (This pope was very free with interdicts and excommunications – it was he who threatened Henry II with the bull for the murder of Thomas à Becket and put the ban on William the Lion of Scotland – and he was also much plagued by anti-popes.) By the time of the third interdict, in 1309, familiarity with the *Anathema sit* had bred contempt in the Venetians. 'Children are terrified by words; valiant men fear not even the sword's point,' said the doge, Pietro Gradenigo. St Mark was as good as St Peter, as far as the Venetians were concerned. They were self-sufficient in their piety. They even had their own saints. San Rocco, for example, whom Venice had canonized but 'the pope not yet,' as Wotton put it.

The moral terrors of the interdict meant nothing to this unsuperstitious people, who only feared for their commerce, which could be preyed upon by Christian nations. During the fourth interdict, in 1481, the Patriarch of Venice pretended to be ill, so as not to have to receive the messenger with the Papal bull. Meanwhile, he secretly informed the Ten, who told him to take no notice of it. The Patriarch obeyed, and masses were said, as usual, in defiance of the pope's orders; children were baptized, and the dying received the sacraments. The first loyalty of the Venetian clergy was to the Republic, and if a cleric forgot this, the Ten were there to remind him. In 1606, a priest who declined to say mass found a gibbet in front of his church – a piece of sign-language which he promptly heeded. Another priest, in Padua, announced that he was waiting for inspiration from the Holy Ghost; the governor told him that the Holy Ghost had already inspired the Ten to hang anyone who disobeyed.

This sample of Venetian humour – dry, sour, and succinct – induced immediate obedience. There were no martyrs, no Thomas à Beckets or Thomas Mores, among the Venetian clergy. Like all true Venetians, they lived in the here-and-now. The pope was in Rome, and God was in Heaven, but *they* were in Venice. The Jesuits, the Theatines, and the Capuchins heeded the interdict and they were expelled from Venetian territory. In the case of the Jesuits, the pretext was welcome, for the Republic frowned on these representatives of the Church Militant, just as it had frowned on the foreign friars who came to stir up trouble, preaching death to the Jews.

Peace and order (better for business) were the watchwords of the Republic, which would not recognize any authority but its own. The Inquisition, with its 'Dogs of God,' was never welcome in Venice. It was admitted only reluctantly and in a modified form, being placed under the supervision of three Venetian citizens, known as the *Savii all' heresia*, whose job was not to sniff out heresy but to protect Venetian citizens from arbitrary actions of the

Holy Office. The Venetians punished priests and monks for immorality, false coining, and other crimes by hanging them in a cage or *cheba*, on a pole stuck out of a window half way up the Campanile. One priest spent a year there in the fifteenth century. These culpable clerics, fed on bread and water, were one of the circus-attractions of the Piazza, competing with the jugglers and mountebanks and the booths selling beads and lace and glassware. Ballads on them were hawked, like the 'Lament of Father Augustine,' condemned to the cage for gambling and blaspheming, and the companion 'Lament of Father Augustine's Woman,' who wishes that she had the wings of a bird, so that she could comfort her forlorn paramour in his aviary on the Campanile.

Such spectacular punishments were not pleasing to the Church, which claimed for itself the right to try ecclesiastics and mete out its own justice. And it was over just such a case, of two 'criminous clerics,' that the storm of 1606 broke, with the monk, Paolo Sarpi, acting as the defender of the secular power. There was also a question of Church property and of taxation involved. When the interdict fell, Wotton, in his palazzo, could not help jubilating, for the break, this time, appeared decisive. A stubborn pope, a stubborn ruler – it was going to be Henry VIII and Clement VII all over again. No Englishman could fail to feel the analogies. *Questa sola repubblica, questo sol angolo d'Italia* had the same independent, seafaring habits as 'this scepter'd isle, this earth of Majesty, this seat of Mars, this other Eden, demi-paradise, this fortress

built by Nature for herself . . . this happy breed of men,
this little world, this precious stone set in the silver sea,
which serves it in the office of a wall' – a description that
could serve as a description of Venice. But the analogy
was incomplete. Wotton could not foresee any possibility
of compromise – which meant that he was not a
Venetian.

The outcome of the interdict, which lasted a year, was a
typically Italian bargain. Venice agreed to surrender the
two criminous clerics to the French ambassador, 'without
prejudice to the doge's right to try ecclesiastics'; the
ambassador turned them over to the French cardinal
Joyeuse, who turned them over to the Church courts,
while the Republic, as it were, looked the other way. In
return, the Church yielded, on the question of taxation and
Church property. Rome, on the whole, had lost, but
Venice remained Catholic.

Yet Wotton was not altogether wrong in seeing the
stuff of martyrs in the satirical Servite. The Curia nursed
its grudge. Months after the settlement, when all was
supposed to be friendly, Sarpi came close to martyrdom,
at the hands of the pope's hired assassins, who set upon him
as he was coming home one evening to his monastery near
Santa Fosca, accompanied only by a lay brother and an
aged nobleman. The streets were empty because the
inhabitants of the district at that hour were – as usual – at
the theatre. Repeated blows were struck at him, and he was
left for dead, with a dagger skewered through his head,
from the right ear to the cheekbone. But he was carried into

his monastery, while some women on a balcony fired harquebuses at the murderers, and eventually he recovered. He was shown the dagger while he still lay between life and death, and he greeted it with a sally as sharp as the weapon itself. 'I recognize the *style* of the Roman Curia,' he observed, in Latin, punning on the word, *stilus*, which means both *style* and *dagger*.

In the same cool spirit, he hung the dagger, as an ex voto, in his monastery church, Santa Maria dei Servi, from which it was removed by Venetian patriots when the church was desecrated by Napoleon. Today what is left of the monastery is an orphanage, kept by nuns. It is not open to visitors. But you can catch a glimpse of a garden behind high ivied walls and a pretty Gothic portal in varicoloured marble. Nearby, in the campo of Santa Fosca, is a rather bad statue of the friar, put up in 1892. At the time of Sarpi's death (at the age of 71), the Senate decreed a monument to him, but the nuncio forbade it as an insult to the pope. The Venetian ambassador gave in, saying: 'He who may not live in stone will live in our annals, with less risk from all-corroding time' – a pious platitude more in the *style* of the Curia than in that of the terse Republic. Besides, it did not turn out to be true.

Sarpi today is a somewhat forgotten figure, no longer the favourite he was, during the nineteenth century, with English and American tourists '*della religione*.' He was essentially a Protestant hero, though like Lord Acton he could never resolve to make the break. But militant Protestantism, which held him in veneration, as the man who defied the pope, is a thing of the past. His statue stands unnoticed in busy Santa Fosca. Fashions change in tourism. It used to be the thing to go to Chioggia and to hear the Greek service at the Chiesa dei Greci and to look for mementoes of Sarpi. Now it is Harry's Bar at Torcello and the Ca' Rezzonico.

I came upon the Servite monastery by accident, being attracted by the high walls and the garden, as I passed along the Rio della Misericordia, in that same northern, unfrequented quarter, with its grey, even, lifeless light, where the Ghetto lies and where the signora's husband is putting up new houses. It is the section of Venice I like best to walk in and contains two lovely Gothic churches, the rosy Madonna dell'Orto, with a beamed wooden ceiling and tall ogival arcades, a wonderful Cima and the Tintoretto 'Presentation of the Virgin' (far surpassing, I think, Titian's in the Academy), and Sant' Alvise, with a painted ceiling in *trompe-l'œil* architectural perspectives, a Tiepolo Crucifixion and the curious knightly pictures called baby-Carpaccios, after Ruskin's attribution. These two small, all-but deserted churches secrete a flowery essence of medieval Venice, still half-oriental and permeated with spice; each of them, odd to say, has a painting of the Golden Calf being worshipped by the Children of Israel. Nearby along a house front are those strange figures on camels called the Moors, thought to represent Levantine merchants who inhabited the quarter. Tintoretto lived in this melancholy region and he is buried in the Madonna dell' Orto. Children are ready to point out his house to you. But when I asked about Sarpi's despoiled convent, for the first time in Venice nobody could supply any information. There were some sisters there, '*suore*' – that was all anyone knew.

'*Esto perpetua*' ('*May it last forever*'). These dying words, attributed to Sarpi, are supposed to refer to the Republic. Just before, delirious, he is said to have muttered: 'I must go to St Mark's. It is late. There is much to do.' These remarks, coming from the only real thinker Venice ever produced, have a somewhat disquieting effect. The Republic, a wholly rational structure, had no interest in reason in its purer forms – only in *applied* reason, as one might say applied science. The subtle Venetian intelligence expended itself in diplomatic '*relazioni*' and practical statecraft. The Venetians printed books but seldom wrote them. Outside of Goldoni, there are no Venetian writers of any consequence. Petrarch left his library to the Republic, in gratitude for the haven it had given him – that 'window' on the Riva from which he looked out on the world's traffic. But the Republic mislaid the books and apparently did not even miss them for 114 years. When Sansovino was put to work building the Libreria Vecchia to house the collection of 900 precious Greek and Latin manuscripts left the Republic seventy years before by Cardinal Bessarion, an embarrassing fact came to light: both libraries had vanished. They found Cardinal Bessarion's, finally, shoved away in an attic above St Mark's portico, but Petrarch's were never recovered. It was a little the same with Sarpi. Venice valued his talents, but it harnessed them to a purpose too narrow for their scope – the service of the State – just as though the Grimani Breviary, preserved in the Libreria Vecchia, were to be thumbed through daily as a doge's private prayerbook.

Sarpi was a rare specimen, certainly, to find rooted in Venice, like one of those flowering plants one sees growing on the bridges – the descendants of tenacious seedlings carried in on the white Istrian stone. His father was a native of mountainous Friuli, the northern Venetian province – a wild place, still, half-Albanian in feeling. His mother was a Venetian, and he was born in Venice. After some time in Mantua (at the court of that same Duke William to whom Veronica Franco, the courtesan, dedicated her terza rima) and a stay in Rome, he came back to Venice to teach philosophy at the Servite convent. He wrote the History of the Council of Trent (much admired by Gibbon), and letters on various topics, scientific, philosophical, and religious. But his main work was done for the Republic, as a volunteer polemicist, so that he is remembered as a local oddity, where he might have been a universal philosopher. He had the philosopher's love of truth and the Venetian's diplomacy. 'I never *never* tell a lie,' he said, 'but the truth not to everybody.' (*'Le falsità non dico mai mai, ma la verità non a ogniuno.'*) He was witty, sarcastic, ceremonious, spare in utterance, dry. He helped Galileo construct the telescope and received an acknowledgment from him to *'mio padre e maestro Sarpi.'* He worked on anatomy and discovered the contraction of the iris. In his treatise on the Art of Thinking Well, he is said to have anticipated Locke's theory of the modes of knowledge.

He was a very thin, almost emaciated man, with a large round forehead, a long bony nose, and black, piercing eyes. His frame, despite its thinness, was heavy-set. His health was poor, and he treated himself with home-made remedies – cassia, manna, and tamarind, the remedies of the peasantry and the poor. He suffered from the cold and used to hold a piece of warm iron in his hands to heat himself. This was one of many peculiar, crankish habits. Wotton, who hoped to make a convert of him, described him sitting in his cell, 'fenced with a castle of paper about his chair and over his head when he was either reading or writing alone, for he was of our Lord of St Alban's opinion that all air is predatory, and especially hurtful when the spirits are most employed.' His cell was very bare. He had a table, a box for his books, a bench, a crucifix above a human skull, a picture of Christ in the Garden, and a little bed, though he preferred to sleep on his book box. His sheets lasted him twenty years.

These stage-properties appear to have come straight out of Venetian painting. Seated at his table, reading or writing, he might have posed for Lorenzo Lotto, that visionary, mystic painter, himself of a Protestant, evangelical turn, who drew his inspiration, as Berenson pointed out, directly from the Bible instead of from official Church legends, and whose figures, somewhat stumpy and ill-favoured, looming out of shadows and lit by a disturbed light, have something Dutch about them – premonitions of Rembrandt. And yet Fra Paolo Sarpi, as Wotton finally saw, had 'much of the Melanchthon but little of the Luther.' There is an element of disquietude, of derangement, in Lotto's work that would not have suited Sarpi's witty, perspicuous mind: Carpaccio, with his realism and faint irony, would have pleased him better. Carpaccio's St Jerome (in San Giorgio degli Schiavoni), surrounded by his statuary, his armillary spheres, his elegant little pots and handsome studded furniture, his books and his music, looking out of the window for literary inspiration while his little white dog patiently watches for it too, this manly, worldly, humanist St Jerome (the one who loved Cicero) did himself better, as the phrase goes, than the Servite friar. But Fra Paolo's paper castle against draughts – one imagines it castellated – is pure Carpaccio. It is the Carpaccio quirk, the crochet, the utilitarian note which becomes fantastic in the setting, like the traffic-light on the canal. We see it in St Ursula's little mules lined up beside her bed in the St Ursula series in the Academy, in the wooden leg of the fleeing monk in the St Jerome series in the Schiavoni Church, in St Jerome's attentive dog, waiting for the light of inspiration to strike, in the damsel's half-eaten camisole – a dainty, lingerie touch – which has just been savoured by the dragon in the St George series on the opposite wall. This signature, so to speak, of Carpaccio's, this reasoned, everyday logic applied to the realm of miracles, is a product of the Venetian artist's lucidity. The critic Roberto Longhi speaks of 'a cruel fanlight of beaten iron in the footlights of the picture' [St George in Combat with the Dragon]. This is the vise of logic in which Carpaccio's fairy world is held – the logic of the paper castle and the piece of warm iron.

With his heavy bones and long nose, Fra Paolo might also have been painted by the stiff Bartolomeo Vivarini of the Murano school, or by Antonio, his more imaginative brother, who might have shown him in his monk's robes, with the dagger through his head, like St Peter Martyr (dear to the painters of Verona and thence all through the Veneto), illustrating the manner of his martyrdom, in the charming, unruffled fashion of the northern Italian saints: St Lucy carrying her eyes, like a *plat du jour*, and St Agatha, her breasts, in a clean white saucer.

But these are all historical impossibilities. The painters I am assigning to Sarpi were dead, long dead, most of them, before Sarpi's time; Lotto, the youngest of them, died, an old man, in Loreto, when Sarpi was a boy of four. Sarpi belonged, in time, to the age of Veronese, whose work 'Supper in the Pharisee's House,' now in the Louvre, had been painted for the refectory of the Servite monastery in 1572. Fra Paolo must have let his eyes rest on it often during his years as Father Provincial. But in temper the vegetarian friar (he lived on vegetables, a little white wine, and toast, touching meat very rarely, because of his delicate palate) was a throwback from Veronese's world of buffoons and goddesses, apes and blackamoors, shining swords and bucklers, ruffs and pearls, parrots and convoluted pillars. Wotton, with his halberds and bucklers, belonged to the Veronese world, certainly; he kept an ape in his palace, collected lutes and Titians, and retired to a villa on the Brenta, like Veronese's people, during the hot spells. The fact is, however, that Veronese was dead when Wotton came to Venice.

He was alive and in full vigour, though, the year Paolo Scarpi came home to teach philosophy at the Servite convent. The previous year (1573), the painter had been in hot water with the Holy Office, which had summoned him to its headquarters, the chapel of St Theodore in St Mark's, to 'explain' the canvas, 'Banquet in the House of Levi,' which he had done for the refectory of the Dominicans at SS. Giovanni and Paolo. (This is the immense Veronese, originally called 'The Last Supper', that now hangs in the Academy.) The Dominican prior had been warned, already, by the Holy Office to have Veronese substitute the Magdalen for a large dog in the foreground. Now the whole composition was offered in evidence against the painter. Veronese defended himself on artistic grounds, but his judges, as is usual in such cases, brushed this explanation aside and searched for a darker motive. 'What is the meaning,' they demanded, 'of those men dressed in German fashion each with a halberd in his hand?' . . . 'Were you commissioned by any person to paint Germans and buffoons and such-like things in this picture?' 'No, my lord . . . ' Why, the investigators continued, had he represented St Peter cutting up a lamb and another apostle using a fork as a toothpick? Veronese answered that he had intended no irreverence. The

Inquisitors let this pass and returned to the original scent. 'Does it appear to you fitting that at Our Lord's last supper you should paint buffoons, drunkards, Germans, dwarfs, and similar indecencies?' 'No, my lord . . .'

The upshot of the trial was that he was ordered to alter the picture at his own expense, within a month. Veronese, however, hit upon a simpler remedy. A true son of the Veneto, he merely changed the title. This shows how little real power the Holy Office had in Venice, especially since the Inquisitors, in a sense, were right. The picture *is* irreligious and quite unsuitable for a Dominican refectory. The reason is not the presence of dwarfs, buffoons, and parrots, but the presence of Our Lord. It is He, conventionally represented, with a sickly halo, who strikes a false note – a note of insincere feeling – in the brilliant Renaissance tableau. This false note is struck regularly in Venetian painting whenever Christ appears – except in Tintoretto and in the Pietàs of Giovanni Bellini and in certain Crucifixions and Depositions.

These are large exceptions, you might say. But in fact, leaving out Tintoretto (who was a special case), they are really but one exception. That is, Crucifixions, Depositions, and Pietàs fall into a single category, in which Christ is no longer a man, but a cadaver or the next thing to it – a writhing mass of tormented flesh. The Venetians were quite equal to the representation of the dead or dying God – on one of his Pietàs, Giovanni Bellini wrote that he painted it weeping – but the idea of a man-God, a living man like themselves who was also divine, constrained them. Naturally, I am not speaking of the Holy Child, whom the Venetians, like all painters, agreed to treat simply as a human baby, but of the Man Christ, as he appears in the various Suppers at Emmaus, Last Suppers, Suppers with the Pharisee, and so on, or defending the Woman Taken in Adultery – a subject which had a special attraction for Venetian painters. In every instance (leaving out Tintoretto), it is the same; the painter is embarrassed by the Figure and either makes Him weak and vapid, with lack-lustre hair and beard and feeble aureole, as is usually the case with Veronese and Titian, or reduces him, as Lotto does, to a sort of woodcut illustration out of some medieval text – Lotto's Christ is always deformed, with short legs and a flattened head that sits square on the body without any neck. The real trouble with Veronese's picture is that Christ, its centre, is hollow.

Paolo Sarpi confessed to Von Dohna, the ambassador of Christian of Anhalt, that he disliked saying mass but did it during the interdict so as not to seem to be yielding to the pope's ban. This is a very frank revelation, from a sincerely religious friar to a layman who wrote everything Sarpi told him to his Lutheran master, who was waiting in Germany to hear which way Venice would go, in religion. The two envoys of the Protestant princes enjoyed Sarpi's complete confidence, but the Lutheran was less sanguine than the English Protestant agent. The facts and figures Sarpi gave Von Dohna to pass on to Germany did not encourage him to hope; Wotton, handing out Bibles, was engrossed in his own successes and did not heed the realities of power. And yet, on Wotton's side, was the fact that the Ten and the Three must have known what Sarpi was up to but did nothing to stop him, when the pope's spies were everywhere, even, as it turned out later, in Sarpi's monastery itself. In the light, moreover, of the intimacy with Von Dohna, the interrogation of Veronese assumes a new aspect. As the Holy Office wanted to know, what were those Germans doing at Christ's Last Supper? Who commissioned them? What did they signify? Were they merely figures of fun, on a par with buffoons, dwarfs, and drunkards – a clown's role they sometimes play, even today, as tourists in a southern land? Or were they 'indecencies' unfit for the occasion because they were heretics? It is curious, certainly, the way the interrogator keeps coming back to the question of those 'Germans,' as though they were the chief or most outrageous offence.

Veronese is usually regarded as the most pagan and joyous of the Venetian painters, and no doubt he added the Germans to Christ's feast, just as he said, for ornament, because they were part of the joy and riot of the world. Nevertheless, it remains odd that he was singled out to be tried by the Holy Office, when all the Venetian painters, from Carpaccio on, were accustomed to people the sacred scene with dogs and cats and birds, as well as dwarfs and other indecencies. And, as Veronese himself pointed out, Michelangelo 'in the Papal Chapel in Rome had painted Our Lord Jesus Christ, His mother, St John and St Peter, and all the court of Heaven from the Virgin downwards, all naked, and in various attitudes, with little reverence.'

That was different, the Inquisitors answered. Those were disembodied spirits. Yet in Tintoretto's 'Last Supper,' painted for the Scuola di San Rocco (the as yet uncanonized saint whose bones the Venetians had got hold of) about fifteen or more years after the trial of Veronese, a large dog appears again and in exactly the same spot on the canvas – the centre foreground, where the Inquisitors had recommended that a Magdalen should stand. This time the Holy Office was not scandalized. Why not, one would like to know.

First, adulation and ceremony; second, Lutheranism; third, debauchery. An impossible combination, one would think. And yet they flourished together in Venice during the last years of the Golden Age – a triumph of coexistence. The Lion lay down with the lamb. Paolo Sarpi's cell, a medieval grotto, was linked to the embassy of a Renaissance gentleman, to the Doge's Palace and the Hall of the Ten, to Veronese's studio, in what must have appeared to the Curia a vast network of conspiracy, a conspiracy the more dangerous for being – to change the figure – hydra-headed, with a subtle, ceremonious monk preaching pietistic doctrines of the simple heart (Sarpi thought God was indifferent to externals and cared only for the heart's faith), while a worldling painter celebrated Christ's communion as a glittering debauch.

The conspiracy, whatever its dimensions, failed. The expedient Republic, fearful of Spanish arms, accepted the

Church's bargain. Wotton, who had been showered with honours by the Republic, soon found it difficult to be received on state-business by the doge. The Jesuits were readmitted. Sarpi, in moments of discouragement, considered that the great fight had been all in vain and wondered whether it would not be best to lay off his habit and take refuge in England, like his friend, De Dominis, another Venetian philosopher-theologian, who discovered the true theory of the rainbow. De Dominis was received with joy and inducted into the Church of England. But Sarpi could not resolve on it. Instead, he concentrated on St Mark's business, hurrying back and forth to the Councils of the Republic, under a covered passageway constructed for him by the city, so that he could reach his gondola without fear of the pope's assassins. De Dominis came to a bad end; he recanted Protestantism, came to Rome with hopes of preferment, and was thrown into prison, where he died. An anathema was pronounced on his body, which was taken from its coffin, dragged through the streets of Rome, and burned in the Campo dei Fioro. While in London he arranged for the publication of Sarpi's *History of the Council of Trent* and appropriated the money James I gave him as a reward to Sarpi for this subversive work.

St Mark's business was better than this. Sarpi remained in his cell, with his picture of The Agony in the Garden – Christ's own ordeal of irresolution – as a comfort or possibly a reproach. One would like to know who painted it. Carpaccio tried this subject in San Giorgio degli Schiavoni. It is the only poor painting in the series. Carpaccio's noonday reason, which flooded all his legends with an almost Voltairean light, shrank from a candid examination of the praying God. '*La verità non a ogniuno.*'

5

The Sands of Time

It was from Byzantium that the taste for refinement and sensuous luxury came to Venice. '*Artificiosa voluptate se mulcebat*,' a chronicler wrote of the Greek wife of an early doge. Her scents and perfumes, her baths of dew, her sweet-smelling gloves and dresses, the fork she used at table scandalized her subjects, plain Italian pioneer folk. The husband of this effeminate woman had Greek tastes also. He began, says the chronicler, 'to work in mosaic,' importing mosaic workers – and marbles and precious stones – to adorn his private chapel, St Mark's, in the Eastern style that soon became second nature to the Venetians.

The Byzantine mode, in Venice, lost something of its theological awesomeness. The stern, solemn figure of the Pantocrator who dominates the Greek churches with his frowning brows and upraised hand does not appear in St Mark's in His arresting majesty. In a Greek Church, you feel that the eye of God is on you from the moment you step in the door; you are utterly encompassed by this all-embracing gaze, which in peasant chapels is often represented by an eye over the door. The fixity of this divine gaze is not punitive; it merely calls you to attention and reminds you of the eternal Law of the universe arching over time and circumstance. The Pantocrator of the Greeks has traits of the old Nemesis, sweetened and purified by the Redemption. He is also a Platonic idea, the End of the chain of speculation.

The Venetians were not speculators or philosophers, and the theological assertion is absent from St Mark's mosaics, which seek rather to tell a Biblical story than to convey an abstraction. The *clothing* of the story assumes, in Venice, an adventitious interest, as in the fluffy furs worn by Salome in the Bapistery mosaic. The best Venetian mosaics are not in St Mark's, the doge's showcase, but in Torcello, which was an episcopal see in its own right and owed political allegiance to the Greek exarchate of Ravenna.

Torcello is supposed to have been founded by a direct order from God to the Bishop of Altinum. This is a legend one can believe. Unlike Venice, which was the product of necessity and invention, Torcello does indeed appear to be the result of a divine imperative. Only God, you feel, would have commanded a city to be set here on this flat, mournful prairie, barely afloat in the marshy lagoons – an island that was abandoned in the more rational eighteenth century because of the noisome malarious vapours that had reduced the population, once numbering 20,000, to a skeleton crew.

Torcello is healthy enough now and a favourite rendezvous with tourists. A private motorboat runs twice a day in season from Harry's Bar *in urbe* to Harry's Bar in Torcello, a pleasant rustic tavern set in a ragged garden, surrounded by festoons of grapevines. You have an hour and a half to lunch or dine on Harry's specialities (lobster and scampi and fish soup and lasagne) and half an hour to inspect the two churches, buy souvenirs and postcards and Burano lace doilies, before being sped back to Venice. There is a boy in the Cathedral who explains the mosaics.

If I sigh over this, it is because I have read the accounts of earlier tourists, who used to cross from Burano by gondola and walk alone on the pestilential island, musing on the fate of civilizations in the mood of Shelley's 'Ozymandias.' That is how Torcello should be seen. But now to the melancholy of its widowed Cathedral and orphaned daughter-church, Santa Fosca, a new, modern element has been added the melancholy of desecration and of the tomb's solitude invaded. All sacred spots today possess this freshened sadness. A double 'Never more' echoes over the tomb of Theodoric at Ravenna, the catacombs, the temple at Sunium, where Byron carved his name. Not being sacred, Venice is happily free from these gloomy reverberations. But once you embark on the lagoons, it is another matter; the voices of guides and of other touristic parties become suddenly insupportable.

It is still possible, however, to go the old way to Torcello, taking the Murano-Burano vaporetto from the Fondamenta Nuova, lunching at Burano, and continuing by gondola to the sluggish canals and reedy landing-place of Torcello. If you dally in Burano long enough, you will miss the Harry's Bar parties, who will be on their way back to Venice, and there will only be the souvenir-vendors and the postcard people and the lace-women and the custodians, lined up to speak to you in a babel of tongues.

Burano is 'a characteristic fishing centre,' the touring club guide book says. Its speciality is lace, and the thing to do, people tell you, is to go after lunch (in a 'characteristic' restaurant, a sort of billiard parlour specializing in sea food and hung with genre studies acquired by the proprietor from artist patrons) to see the lace made in the Scuola dei Merletti down the street. It is upstairs, on the second floor of a little ogival city hall, this institution: a long double room, with rather poor light, where silent rows of little girls in smocks sit on benches, presided over by a nun and a crucifix, pricking out lace for the Society of the Jesurum, a pious, charitable group of worthy ladies who pay the children 400 lire (64 cents, about the same wage they received in 1913) for an eight-hour day making Burano or point de Venise that will sell for very high prices in Venice, in the Society's shop on the Rio della Canonica near the Bridge of Sighs.

I will not vouch for these figures. They were supplied by an angry Burano gondolier, who may well have been a Communist. There are plenty of hammers and sickles on the Venetian red housefronts of Burano, as in the scabious lagoon towns of the Chioggia itinerary – Malamocco, San

Pietro in Volta, Pellestrina. But I believed the gondolier because what he said matched the ferocious looks in the eyes of the children as they passed their hoops of needlework up to the floorwoman for us to marvel over. We came in, smiling, a group of three, exclaiming to ourselves mentally, 'What a charming scene!' But when we tried to shower these smiles on the children, not a muscle moved in their faces; only the raised eyes shot looks like poisoned darts.

Yes, said the gondolier, the eyesight was often affected; many could not work after a few years in the lace school. 'Who is responsible?' 'Who gets the money?' we demanded. A lady in Venice, he said promptly: the Contessa Margherita. I was eager to see this 'Contessa Margherita,' whom I imagined as belonging to the chipper smart set that appears every Sunday, like a covey of birds, for a pre-lunch apéritif at Florian's, sitting at the far end, near the Bocca di Piazza. But in fact there is no such person. The old queen Margherita, long since dead, was once a patroness of the Society. Who actually profits I have never been able to find out. The signora, who knows everything, does not know; the head of the Venetian gondoliers' co-operative, a veteran anti-fascist with a halo of white hair, does not know. Everyone I ask is vague. I went back to Burano one day to check my first impression, which remained unaltered. And I have found the Burano lace school a useful touchstone for judging the authors of travel books on Venice. There are those like E. V. Lucas, in *A Wanderer in Venice*, published in 1914:

'Yet there is an oasis of smiling cleanliness, and that is the chief sight of the place – the Scuola Merletti, under the patronage of Queen Margherita . . . thousands of girls, pretty girls too, some of them, with their black massed hair and olive skin and all so neat and happy. Specimens of their work, some of it of miraculous delicacy, may be bought and kept as a souvenir of a delightful experience.'

A different age, you might say, but here is André Maurel in *Quinze Jours à Venise*, published the same year:

'*Ce n'est pas ici la tristesse de l'usine. Mais peut-être plus pénible encore. Hôpital, orphelinat, ouvroir, asile, de pauvres d'esprit? C'est un peu tout cela à la fois, l'atelier des dentelles à Burano, sans tragique, mais d'une faiblesse qui apitoie infiniment . . . Il n'est pas bon de remonter à la source du luxe . . . La religieuse qui dirige les filles me dit que certaines arrivent à gagner des trois et quatre francs par jour. Après combien d'années d'affaissement sur la taille, de tête courbée, de pauvres yeux perdus?*'

Fortunately, Burano has less daunting sights to offer. In the church of San Martino, in the sacristy, there is an early Tiepolo 'Crucifixion,' which is like a ghastly masquerade ball, with banners and swirling draperies and late-Goya faces and peering, deformed wretches in stage rags. The swooning virgin wears a dainty shirred morning cap and a red gown. In the background, there are clown figures in chalky grisaille with leering swollen lips and potato noses. It is a more theatrical vision than that of the Madonna dell' Orto 'Crucifixion,' with its transfiguring light; yet it shares with it a kind of terror, a sense of the day when the veil of the Temple was riven, that suggests that Tiepolo was not so devoid of feeling as some recent critics assert.

The same sacristy has a charming Mansueti 'Flight into Egypt,' which swarms with odd fancies too, though of a humbler kind. A domestic, Italian donkey with his precious burden toils through a landscape that is alive with exotic birds, both real and imaginary, as well as lions and tigers.

Along the side-streets of Burano, you see groups of old black-shawled women sitting on chairs in the sun in front of the low houses, making lace. No doubt, these are the apprentices of Maurel's day. Now that they are old, it does not seem to matter. Their eyes are past harming, if they have kept them this long, and the trade is a sociable one, suited to the habits of declining years. Bead-stringing is also a speciality with the Burano old wives, who like to have you watch them as they stand in their open kitchens, poking a long wire into a dish of white beads and bringing it up, strung, after a rapid, dexterous stirring motion, as if with an egg whisk. This legerdemain is the home counterpart of the glass-blowing feats of nearby Murano. Burano is cheerful because so much takes place outdoors here, in the sunlight. There seem to be no secrets. The first sight that meets the visitor's eye as he arrives on the vaporetto is the whole town's laundry blowing in the breeze, a banner welcome, in the green public park at the quayside.

During the fall, big chunks of hot roasted winter squash – a rough Burano delicacy – are sold from barges in the canals. The Burano barge men are dark and wild-looking, with great moustaches, like Sicilians. When they make the trip to Venice, they anchor their boat under one of the bridges and eat and sleep there – in public. For several days in November, one of these boats spent the night under my bridge. Coming home after dark, I would see the glowing stove and the lantern lighting up the figure of an old man peeling potatoes under the shadow of the bridge against the black canal water. It was a primitive, almost an aboriginal sight, an apparition in worldly Venice from Vulcan's ancient forge. The Buranese fishermen and boatmen are aware of how different they are from the slender, fragile, civilized Venetians – how picturesque and brawny. A group of them, all sooty, rows under the Academy bridge, waving and roaring and flashing their teeth up at us, like circus strong men. They have the reputation of being very handsome, but they are not. The poverty of the island has misshapen most of them, squinted their eyes, pocked their skins, and left them short of teeth

Burano is a good approach to Torcello, for one is going by stages, backward in time. Venice is an eternal present; Burano is the nineteenth century, operatic, vivid, with ragged coloured sails in the canals, nets being mended, roasting squash, emerald-green water, and yellow and white houses. You step off the vaporetto straight into an old-fashioned opera setting, with a cast of characters and a chorus provided by the local trades; there is even a villainess in the wings, the 'Contessa Margherita,' a contralto part, who will arrive from Venice in her laces and silks. The poverty of Burano is the 'happy poverty' dear to the nineteenth century: rags and sunlight and an artist with a flowing necktie sketching the scene.

Chioggia is a different story. Chioggia is the nineteenth century in its miserable aspect. I went there one day on a motorboat in a pearl-grey fog – a sinister excursion past a chain of islands that encloses Venice like a *cordon sanitaire*: the island of the contagious-disease hospital, the island of the tuberculous hospital, the island of the female insane, the island of the male insane. (And it is along here, I have discovered, that Wotton's Orphans' Canal runs – the executioner's oubliette.) These islands and the wretched lagoon towns strung out along the Lido and Pellestrina are haunted by legends of the remote past – of the repulse of Pepin, of the repulse of the Huns – and by stories of ghosts and miraculous visitations. Here were the original, imperilled settlements, before the move to Rialto in the ninth century, and here begin the hammers and sickles of today.

Chioggia must have had a different look before they filled in the main canal, so that automobiles can drive down the broad grey main street. In the old photographs it is like a bigger Burano and it was famous for its rough humours, out of which Goldoni made *Le Baruffe Chioz-zotte*. Now on a grey, foggy day, it is the picture of dereliction. The sails are beautiful, with their curious mystic designs, roses and crescents and cups, in yellow, orange, blue, and watermelon pink, but the town is fly-specked and mangy. The buildings are all peeling; the communal watertaps drip; the paintings are rotting in the gloomy churches. The cats are so thin that they look like a single bone with fur draped loosely around it. The inhabitants are no longer the weatherbeaten, bloused banditti that one sees in the old photographs, but greyfaced city denizens, wearing cheap business clothes. The whole town is like a big, secretive nineteenth-century tenement or warehouse on which hammers and sickles have been scrawled.

It was the scene of the great naval victory of the Venetians over the Genoese in the fourteenth century, when the Venetians, under their intrepid admiral, Vettor Pisani, released from jail for the emergency by popular demand, blockaded the blockaders within the port of Chioggia and waited anxiously for relief from the erratic captain, Carlo Zeno, coming from God knew where – Crete or the Bosporus. This is the one heroic moment in Venetian history, a long tense moment in which calculation was forgotten and everything was left to fate. Here, uniquely for Venice, individual character marked an event; Carlo Zeno was a bankrupt gambler and troubadour who had been wandering over Europe as a soldier of fortune;

Pisani was a choleric patriot, simple, impulsive, athletic, and quick with his fists. Each of these two patricians was reckless in his own way; each was a popular idol and suspect to the oligarchy. As usual, there was a peace party in Venice that favoured compromise or surrender, and Pisani was allowed till January 1, 1380, to continue the counter-blockade; if Zeno did not arrive by then, Pisani agreed to give up his strategy, and starving Venice would submit to the hereditary enemy. This fairy-tale bargain had a fairy-tale ending. At dawn on January 1, after more than two months of suspense, five sails were sighted on the horizon, too far distant for the eye to make out whether they were friend or foe. Scouts were sent out in small boats and they watched while a flag was hoisted. The Lion of St Mark unfurled. The impossible had happened; Carlo Zeno had got the message. Or, as the historian Hazlitt put it, losing his professional restraint: 'IT WAS CARLO ZENO WHO HAD COME AT LAST; AND VENICE WAS INDEED SAVED.'

The Chioggians themselves took no part in this valorous dream, their town having fallen to the Genoese, who with the help of the Carraresi of Padua sacked it cruelly. The decline of Chioggia dates from this episode. It made a brief sortie into history at the time of the Risorgimento when the Chioggian sailors helped Garibaldi, who was trying to reach Venice, escape from the Austrians into the Ravenna pine forest. The smell of the past is sour here in

Chioggia, like rancid pee of the crouching lion on the pillar by the harbour, the lion the Venetians say is a cat.

But Chioggia is a long way from Torcello, which lies on the other side of Venice in the northern lagoons. Torcello is only a few minutes from Burano, however. One steps out of the gondola into the pioneer days of the lagoon. On this flat, treeless island, with its low, desultory vineyards and stretches of meadow grass, broken vertically only by the Cathedral and the tall isolated bell-tower, one is awesomely conscious of history, for the first time in the Venetian ambience. Indeed, there is nothing else here: only the Cathedral, with the little octagonal church of Santa Fosca close beside it, like a nursling, the bell-tower (closed), the provincial museum, a house or so, a Devil's Bridge with a legend attached to it, a few fishermen and museum custodians, and, of course, Harry's Bar. It is easy to imagine the first settlers arriving here on a little boat, led by their bishop with a cross. The little boat, the vast Cathedral – this is the measure of their piety.

Torcello is said to have been named for the tower in Altinum where the bishop was vouchsafed his vision, when he was seeking refuge for his flock from the savage, heretic Lombards. The idea of height seems essential to this tiny island, which must have figured in its own eyes as a lighthouse of faith and a lookout-point for dangers. The flight of the faithful took place in 638, though in fact some earlier settlers had fled here from Attila in 452. Nothing remains of this first settlement, which may have been impermanent. But Bishop Paul took his see with him from ravaged Altinum, and the Cathedral to S. Maria Assunta (again the idea of height) was erected the next year, in 639. It was modified twice, finally in 1008, but it kept its original form, that of the Ravenna churches, and, standing in tall grass, it still diffuses the early-Christian aura of the Exarchate, of Ravenna's San Vitale and Sant' Apollinare in Classe, which once too looked over a harbour, now silted in and covered with that lonely pine forest where Dante and Byron poeticized and Garibaldi hid.

No building in Venice is as old as this. St Mark's, in the Ravenna style, was begun in 829, but it was twice destroyed, burned down once by the people in rebellion against a tyrannous doge, restored, and torn down again by an eleventh-century doge who wanted his chapel in the fashionable Byzantine style. (It was his successor, Doge Selvo, that married the Greek wife.) The present St Mark's, in the shape of a Greek cross with five domes and modelled, some think, on the church of the Twelve Apostles in Constantinople, is the result of his initiative. The Venetian passion for building had its destructive side. When the Doge's Palace was partly destroyed by fire in the sixteenth century, a commission of architects was consulted, and Palladio counselled tearing down what was left and building a new one. If it had not been for the counter-advice of the Florentine Sansovino, who was more of a trimmer, the Doge's Palace today would be in the Palladian style and a wonder of the world would be lost. The church of San Geminiano (whose destruction brought down the Pope's interdict) was repeatedly torn down; its position in St Mark's Square was unlucky for it. Sansovino's San Geminiano, the last of its line, was demolished by Napoleon to create the Fabbrica Nuova, where the Correr Museum is now located.

The pope had some reason to be angry, for the old church was believed to go back to the sixth century, to Narses the Eunuch who ruled Italy from Ravenna for the Emperor Justinian and had made use of Venetian transport for his armies in his campaign against the Goths. He was one of the first foreigners to be struck by Venetian prosperity. According to tradition, Narses built two churches on what is now the Piazza in fulfilment of a vow: San Geminiano, which he ornamented with marble columns and precious stones, and the more modest church of St Theodore, later swallowed up by St Mark's, like its patron and his crocodile. A still earlier church, San Jacopo di Rialto, is supposed to have been put up on the site of a shipyard in the fifth century. But the present San Giacometto di Rialto (open one day a year), which claims to be that church, is really an eleventh or twelfth century creation, much restored and rebuilt, the last time in the seventeenth century.

The Venetians are enthusiastic restorers. The paintings of the Doge's Palace have been worked on by gangs of restorers ever since the eighteenth century. That is perhaps why, at least to my eyes, they look so verveless; even Tintoretto's great blue circling 'Paradise' is a disappointment, close up – I prefer the cartoon for it in the Louvre. Except for the Veronese 'Industry' with her marvellous spider web on the ceiling of the Sala del Collegio and Tintoretto's 'Marriage of St Catherine' in the same room, Tiepolo's 'Neptune Offering Venus the Gifts of the Sea' on an easel in the Sala delle Quattro Porte and the bonneted figure of the Doge Grimani in the large semi-Titian in the same room, these yards of paint and canvas seem dead and honorific. A better idea of these masters can be formed in the Scuole and the churches, long neglected by the restorers, or in the Academy, which got most of its paintings during the nineteenth century from private collections, or in the various small museums – the Correr, the Querini Stampalia, the Ca' Rezzonico – which were themselves private collections until recent years.

As every visitor knows, only one original mosaic – the left-hand one – has survived on St Mark's façade. The others are 'restorations.' A less advertised fact is that the Torcello mosaics have been restored too, particularly the 'Universal Judgment.' I myself would never have noticed this, had I not been told. But it pains more expert people, who say that it has lost its depth and sparkle, which were due to the uneven setting of the old tiles. The whole Cathedral and Santa Fosca too have undergone restorations; their baroque ornaments have been stripped from them and some new brick has been laid in, to give them once again their bare, primitive aspect. I do not find this objectionable here on Torcello, for the restoration only emphasizes a truth about these churches, which is that life has fled from them.

You pay your admission and enter the Cathedral. In the depths of the church, behind the altar, high up, is the Virgin against a gold background. Facing her, on the entrance wall, is the 'Universal Judgment'. A solemn confrontation, thinks Ruskin, and in theory it ought to be: the Last Things – death, resurrection, immortality, judgment – confront the First Thing – the mystery of the Incarnation. But the real effect is quite different. You must turn your back on the Virgin to look up at the Universal Judgment (12th century, Venetian, Byzantine iconography), and this wheeling has a significance, certainly not intended, but nonetheless real.

The Universal Judgement is arranged in five tiers, with the Crucifixion above and a praying Madonna in the lunette over the door: the Descent into Limbo; Christ in Glory with the Madonna and Saints; the Resurrection of the Body; the Elect separated from the Damned; Bliss and Eternal Fire. It is a solemn arraignment, and the huge mosaic at first sight is awe-inspiring, as the Greek mosaics are. But the Christ in Glory, which should, in the Greek notion, be the radiant centre of the story, is the most perfunctory of the panels. Interest is dispersed to the 'amusing' aspects of the narrative: the Angel, on the right-hand side of the third panel, with the Last Trump, represented as a sort of tuba-horn, and his companion Angels with flutes, blowing a summons to a pagan Nereid, in bracelets and anklets and head-dress, to release the manikin bodies that have been devoured by man-eating fish and spotted sea-serpents and other monsters of the sea, while, on the left-hand side, two land-based Angels pipe to the Lion, king of beasts, seated outside his cave, to order his minions to cough up their half-devoured prey; the damned, in the fourth panel, being chivied into hell, where the devil, a hoary grandfather in blackface, sits dandling a soul on his lap, while the Elect, across the way, look on, like spectators at a sporting event. In the bottom panel, Eternal Fire, with its curly flames licking naked old debauchees, diverts attention from Bliss; in the top panel, majesty is sacrificed to the spectacle of a reluctant, protesting, unregenerate Adam in a white beard being pulled along by a stern Redeemer, Who is obliged to use force to get the old fellow out of his soft life in Limbo.

All this is orthodox theology. The Last Trump does indeed call for the Resurrection of the Body – 'all those whom the flood did and fire shall o'er throw' – and one of the pleasures of the blessed will be to look down over the banisters into hell and watch the damned being tortured. Yet one cannot help smiling over this mosaic, because the Venetian concreteness and visualizing power has turned eschatology into a quirkish folk legend that is not far from the novelistic tales of Carpaccio. The tuba-horn, the costumed Nereid, the spotted sea serpent sitting up like an obedient Fido with his victim between his jaws – these lively details, in bright, clear colours, red and white and turquoise, are pure Venetian fantasy, which is always an extension of Venetian common sense and logic.

All that is left of Byzance in this mosaic is the stupendous size of it, the monitory figure of the Redeemer with his cross, and the two hieratic Archangels in Oriental dress on either side of the top panel. And, of course, the ladies' fashions.

Once you turn round to face the altar, however, the joyous literalness of Venice is behind you. A very different atmosphere emanates from the luminous white-washed basilica, with its three simple naves, carried on eighteen Greek columns with leafy white marble capitals. Ruskin compared it to an ark, and indeed there is that feeling about it: a sense of a covenant between God and the early settlers, with the bishop, as Ruskin says, being their pilot – a common early Christian conception. A marine light flows in through the high, rude windows, and the Nereid and the denizens of the deep are just behind you. Representation is kept to a minimum, and all attention is directed by the ushering columns to the plain stone altar, literally a table, and to the gold vault above, which symbolized the celestial light. Against this gold background, on a kind of rug-like platform stands the mosaic Virgin, a sober figure in a dark blue fringed dress, holding the Child in one arm while the other is folded stiffly against her breast. She is very thin, compressed to a narrow, sad reminder, a dark, single exclamation point on the empty

gold vault. Her expression is strict – more than that, forbidding, as though she were the superior of a harsh,
penitential order. Even this is not strong enough; her
expression is accusatory.

Below her there is a band of Apostles in the Ravenna
style. In the right side-chapel, there are some charming
early mosaics, of angels with a lamb; in the main nave is
a lovely bas-relief of lions and peacocks; in the right nave,
Attila's Chair, said to be the seat from which the tribunes
administered justice under the Exarchate. The church also
contains the bones of St Heliodorus, first bishop of Altinum,
and an inscription, the earliest in Venetian history, noting
the foundation of the Cathedral in the names of the
Emperor Heraclius and Isaac the Exarch.

What remains most haunting, however, is that strange
figure of the Virgin, small and slender and taut, like a
severe little statue raised up to a great height. She is not
Byzantine, despite her austerity. Nor is she Ravennate, if
there is such a word. She is officially enrolled as a 'capo-
lavoro' of the Venetian school. Yet there is nothing like her
in Venice, and her sad, accusing gaze seems to be fixed on
the Venetian caprices of the 'Universal Judgment' – half
a century earlier – as if in condemnation. She appears, an
isolated perpendicular, to be a peculiar place-spirit of
Torcello, a sobering, unwavering beacon in the empty
Cathedral, itself a lighthouse of an extinguished faith.

Something of this obstinate faith survives in the red-
haired boy who explains the mosaics. He heard me one
afternoon explaining them myself to a friend, and it cannot

have been professional rivalry that caused him to interrupt. 'After the Crucifixion,' I was saying, 'Christ is supposed to have gone down to Limbo – .' 'Not "supposed"; 'E *did*,' the boy cut in, peremptorily. This was a disconcertingly far cry from the Venetian sacristans with their '*Che bello*,' '*Che luce*,' etc. Torcello is 'something different,' as the tourists say to each other. Ruskin's notion of medieval Venice, '*città apostolica e santa*,' receives support from Torcello, just as the operatic conception of Venice as a northern Naples receives support from Burano and Chioggia, while the glass-blowing town of Murano, with its ogival palaces, arches, arcades, and porticoes, proffers a glimpse of the sybaritic Renaissance Venice that was a kind of specious 'Florence in-exile'. Bembo and Tasso and Aretino lived on Murano; it was a breezy garden retreat for humanist gentlemen, who collected art-objects and rare botanical specimens, engaged in Platonic dialogues, and perused Greek and Latin volumes in fine Venetian bindings. Murano was a sort of 'folly' and fell into decline in the seventeenth century; it was revived as an industrial town at the end of the nineteenth century, when the glass-industry made a comeback. That is the eerieness of the lagoons; Venice is ringed by a series of dead cities, each representing a Venetian *possibility* that aborted.

6

The Return of the Native

The Renaissance came late to Venice. Giotto had been dead nearly a hundred years when Jacopo Bellini, returned in 1429 from a sojourn in Florence, opened his atelier at San Geminiano and offered lessons in the Florentine 'way.' Jacopo was equipped with a set of perspective boxes in which he strung little figures of wax and cotton – an innocent, amateur's device to assure obedience to the rules laid down in Tuscany for correctness of perspective. Such mechanical aids to correctness remained popular in Venice. A hundred years later, Tintoretto constructed toy houses in which to try out effects of light and shade – a vulgar stage-director, the critic Longhi calls him, cranking away at his thunder-machine, his rain-machine, his lightning-machine . . . He also made use of a collection of casts from the antique and from Michelangelo.

In Padua, to which the pioneer Jacopo removed, his contemporary, the pedant Squarcione, was teaching the lessons of the antique from a collection of ancient Greek and Roman statues, reliefs, and fragments. This classicizing of Squarcione's had a narrow aim: the correctness of ornament. His pupils went beyond him. The flowers and fruit and columns of the Paduan school, the thrones and architectonic details are decorative, 'antiqued' frames for perspective paintings of the harshest realism: the 'graphic' figures of Mantegna, his gelid dead Christs and harrowed, harrowing crone Madonnas, weeping big tears as hard as rocks.

All this was humanized in Venice, by Mantegna's brother-in-law, Jacopo's illegitimate son, 'manly John Bellini,' as Ruskin was fond of calling him, thus making him into a sort of honorary Englishman. Yet the adjective is right. Giovanni Bellini was a true manly type, sweet and sensitive, yet stalwart in his feeling, an ideal citizen of the pacific Republic, living to a vast old age, working and learning to the very last, like some humble craftsman, apprenticed first to the Gothic-Byzantine tradition, then to Mantegna and his school, then to Piero and to the Van Eyck oil process, and finally to his young pupil, Giorgione, whom he began to learn from when he had passed his seventieth year. In his long life span, extending well into the sixteenth century, he embodied, phylogenetically, the successive stages, from early dawn to full morning, of that New Day which was the Venetian Renaissance.

The Van Eyck secret came to Venice from Flanders via Naples, carried by a Sicilian, Antonello da Messina. Venice had been a way-stop for migratory artists even before Jacopo opened his school. The city was full of Greeks – colonies of mosaic-workers and those madonna-makers of whom El Greco, the Cretan, much later, was one. There were the Slavs who gave their name to the Riva degli Schiavoni and who introduced – with Gregorio Schiavone and Antonio da Negroponte – a slightly Russian note into Venetian painting. In Jacopo Bellini's time, a Lombard colony of architects and sculptors, the family known as the 'Lombardi,' had started building churches and chapels and funerary monuments and the new marble palaces with discs of porphyry and serpentine that made such an impression on Philippe de Commines. Uccello had been in Venice, working on the Chapel of the Mascoli in St Mark's. Guariento, from Padua, had painted frescoes (of which a few burnt fragments remain) for the Doge's Palace. Masolino tramped through on his way to Hungary and gave a few lessons to Antonio Vivarini, who had a workshop in Murano with his brother, Bartolomeo. Dürer was in Venice twice and found the old Giovanni Bellini 'still the best painter' on his second trip. In Giorgione's time, Leonardo came.

Giotto had been in Padua, doing the frescoes for the Capella Scrovegni. Donatello was there, doing the great equestrian statue of the Venetian condottiere, Gattamelata – a Renaissance image of power that stood in the public square like a Trojan horse, from which would issue the mailed Mantegna and his followers, after the break with Squarcione. (This statue excited the envy of the Bergamask condottiere, Colleone, who left the Republic 100,000 sequins in his will if they would build him a monument in the Piazza San Marco. The Republic cheated the dead soldier and had the prideful statue put up in the square of

SS. Zanipolo, by the *Scuola* di San Marco.) To the Murano school of the Vivarini came a certain German, Giovanni d'Alemagna, who worked with Antonio for the nuns of San Zaccaria and the Carità, doing charming Gothic saints for gilded wooden settings. In Padua, this retarded pair engaged in a power struggle with the young Mantegna for the decoration of the Church of the Eremitani; they completed the four Evangelists in the vault and withdrew.

The defeat of the Muranese was inevitable; they bowed to the march of progress. This reflected the inferior role the Venetians had been playing in all the arts but mosaic. Their ogival architecture was too foreign to impress the Renaissance world, except by its richness of decoration. They had never learned fresco, in which the Tuscans excelled. The Gothic breezes that had wafted across the mountains from Avignon and Flanders and up from Emilia and the Marches had not been strong enough to exorcise the prevailing Byzantinism. Icon-makers and mosaicists they remained, in their hearts, arrested in a motionless magnificence: an iconostasis. Even when they were Gothicizing or yielding to a Burgundian-like chivalry, as in Jacobello del Fiore, who glues gold accessories – ribbon rosettes – onto his fashion-plate Archangel, the oriental fixity prevails. Jacobello's gilded arabesques belong to architecture rather than painting; they are like the lacy fenestration of the palazzi on the Grand Canal, which were also heavily gilded before time had its way with them.

The Venetian fascination with gold made them look on

everything as a surface, to which gold could be applied and which could be made to glitter in the dazzling, water-refracted light. The love of deep space and volumes, a natural sentiment with the other Italians, deriving from their geography, with its serene bowls of space in the plains of Lombardy and Umbria and Apulia, did not exist primordially in Venice, which had no space, only a thin snake of a Canal to mirror decorated façades. Many European travellers are shocked by the Venetian indifference to how their buildings look from the back – Longhena's Salute, for instance, which was designed to complete the 'view' from the Piazzetta, horrifies the architectural purist, as the slummy rear views of the palazzi repel American puritan housewives. Venice is not made to be seen in the round.

Venetian architecture, indeed, is stage architecture, caring little (up to Palladio) for principles and concerned mainly with 'effects'. Venice is the world's loveliest city, but it produced only one architect – Palladio – who worked along conceptual lines. Intellectual power, the posing and solving of architectural problems, is missing from Venetian buildings, which captivate the eye by tricks and blandishments, as Venice's detractors have readily perceived. The Florentines were intellectuals, and the Venetians were not. Early in the Renaissance, the Venetians became conscious of this deficiency; they invited Florentine humanists to take up residence in the Republic; they printed Florentine books; and later, in the sixteenth century, they made use of a somewhat degraded Florentine, Jacopo Tatti, called Sansovino, known for his lack of

architectural principle, to revamp the city in High Renaissance style. There are fifteen churches and public buildings
in Venice done in whole or in part by Sansovino, among
them some of the most famous: the Mint, the Old Library,
the Loggetta in the Piazza San Marco, the Scala d'Oro
(possibly), the Bank of Italy on the Grand Canal, the Ca'
Grande, San Francesco della Vigna. Sansovino's work has
been deplored for its lack of conscience, its almost servile
adaptiveness to Venetian love of show. But who, except a
purist, would say that the old Venetians were mistaken in
hiring such a pliable instrument? Sansovino was just the
man for them. The frail shell of Venice could hardly have
stood the weight of a Brunelleschi, an Alberti, a Bramante.
Even Palladio is a little more than the floating city could
take. His best work is in the villas of the Veneto, where the
natural order of sloping hills and fields and vineyards,
ruled into symmetry by centuries of Italian husbandry,
could form a spatial harmony with the classical orders. The
Palladian churches of Venice itself, particularly San
Giorgio Maggiore, are disappointing when examined
closely; they require mist or sunset or night-illumination
– tricks of stage make-up – to work their illusion, which is
that of a mirage or iridescent bubble seen across the water.
You cannot make a silk purse out of a sow's ear. Venice seems
to exist to confound such universal maxims. The Florentines, who were incapable of ruling themselves, produced a
great theorist of government: Machiavelli. The Venetians
had no theorists and evolved a model Republic.

The best of the Venetian trecentists – Paolo Veneziano –
is the most Byzantine among them. Whatever is 'Venetian'
in his severe, formally elegant, compressed, almost biting
works is a sort of super-Byzantinism, a refinement of taste
that surpasses Byzantium. A piece of striped material –
Santa Clara's cloak – catches one's eye in the Academy
polyptych. 'Venetian dress goods,' one says to oneself. But
the cold, passionate taste that chose to dramatize those
incisive horizontals had no counterpart in the West. His
successor, Lorenzo Veneziano, adds some coarse, ruddy
notes from Emilia to an insipid Byzantinism that is not
more advanced for being blond. In the next century,
Antonio Vivarini blows out the cheeks of his madonnas
and female saints and blondines their hair till they resemble
Flemish maidens; yet they are arranged in static, vertical
order, like a Byzantine empress and her train of compan-
ions. Antonio's ventures into the Renaissance ('St Catherine knocking down the idol of Bacchus') took place
under the dizzy spell of the vertical: tall columns and
colonnades and ladders and exquisite, elongated pleats of
drapery create a narrow height without depth.

The happiest works of Jacopo Bellini are not his 'inno-
vations,' like the Correr 'Crucifixion,' where groups of
Giotto-like mourning women and bearded Oriental sages
are submitted to the New Look in perspective, but those
fresh-coloured flat Madonnas, half medieval Florentine,
half Byzantine, like the rose and black 'Virgin with
Child' in the Academy. There is something of the minia-
turist in Jacopo, as there was in his son, Gentile, who

travelled to Turkey and painted portraits of the sultan and his court; the Persian miniaturists liked his style, and a copy of a Gentile Bellini, 'Portrait of a Man Painting,' can be found among the miniatures of the Herat school.

(That curious twinning appears again with the painters. There are three Bellinis, three Vivarinis, two Tintorettos, father and son, four – at least – Bassanos, Palma Vecchio and Palma Giovane, two Longhis, two Tiepolos, Canaletto and his nephew, Bellotto, two Riccis, two Guardis, three Caliaris – one of whom was the painter we know as Veronese, four Vecellis – one of whom was the painter we know as Titian. These painting 'firms' – and there were family firms of sculptors also – were something unique in Italy, at least on such a scale. *Bellini and Sons, Tintoretto and Son, Longhi and Son,* reliable companies turning out a high-quality brand product, like the jewellers and glass-blowers, proclaim the business-like character, the conservatism, of Venetian civilization.)

Jacopo's career, like his perspective boxes, reveals a certain hesitancy, a lack of assurance. Up to Titian, timidity and cautious modesty characterize the Venetian painters, even the hardiest of them: Giovanni Bellini, Carpaccio, Big George (Giorgione) of Castelfranco. This bashfulness is one of their charms. Venetian painting slowly awakes, like a virgin forest awakening. A bright bird jumps off the lap of a stiff Madonna; a flower blooms in the *hortus conclusus*; a rabbit hops in; waterfowl crane their necks; peacocks come down from friezes and begin to promenade. Oxen and lambs appear grazing on the slopes of religious paintings, behind the enthroned Madonna and her palace-guard of saints. It is the stealthy birth of landscape painting.

Landscape, for the Tuscan, is deep space, a vista, a natural 'perspective,' telescopic distance emphasizing the solidity of the windowed room looking out into it. For the Marches painter, it tends, rather, to be a decorated green carpet on which gauzy apparitions play. For the Umbrian, it is one or the other. For Mantegna and the Paduan school, it is a calcified, precipitous terrain, banded, sometimes, with shrubbery, and topped by a ruined fossil-town, toward which a few tiny figures are ascending. Giovanni Bellini took the Mantegna landscape and put it, so to speak, to pasture, as Padua itself, the lair of ferocious individualist despots – the monstrous Ezzelino da Romano, lieutenant of Frederick II, and the Carraresi, famed for their cruelties – submitted to the mild yoke of the commercial Republic.

With the Venetians, thanks to Giovanni Bellini, Nature is alive, a scene of activity, dotted with flocks and hermits' cells, watered by streams, and crowned with knightly castles. A Bellini landscape background is at once ideal and practical, a heavenly vision of terrestrial husbandry, crossed by a mounted knight who has killed the last dragon. A Bellini Virgin, with her full, drooping, pensive eyelids, sits modestly holding up the Child on a marble throne hung with precious fabrics and studded with gems. At her feet, on the throne's carpeted steps, page-boy angels entertain her on their lutes with madrigals, a music of the spheres that echoes sweetly over the earth that can be glimpsed just behind her. Those faraway peaks are a blur as gold revelation of paradise. The roles are reversed. Heaven is located on this world, somewhere on the hills near Asolo, and the Virgin on her throne is not joyful in her majesty but faintly sad.

This glimpse of fecund Nature behind a sacred scene is all the devout Bellini permits in the paintings he did so often that they seem to contain the quintessence of Bellini: the various Madonnas of the Academy, the SS Christopher, Jerome, and Augustine' in San Giovanni Crisostomo, the 'Madonna and the Doge Barbarigo' in San Pietro Martire in Murano, the 'Madonna with Saints' of San Francesco della Vigna. But in mid-career, for a brief period, he pulled aside the veil and confronted Nature, in all her expanse, with the drama of a Transfiguration or a Resurrection or a Pietà. The earth, illuminated by the light of the sacred incident, like a witness forced to testify, becomes poignant in its ordinary routines, as the Virgin was, seated in glory, or in her ring of red cherubim.

In one of his late works, the 'Virgin with Saints' in San Zaccaria, the door has been shut on the kingdom of earth and the heavenly company is meditating in a marble room, each profoundly absorbed in his own thoughts.

Earth is the primal matter of Cima, the son of a hides-dealer from hilly Conegliano in the rustic Veneto. His square-jawed peasant Madonnas reveal their natural origin in the peculiar whitish clayey tones of their complexions, hard baked from the Maker's kiln. This sweet shepherd among Venetian painters ('Virgilian,' Longhi calls him, likening his countryside to the classic *rus* of the Georgics) turns the pure mountain light on the Bellini landscape and figures, which seem to jump forward as if in a stereopticon. Cima's golden, crystal light is that of the Veneto in the autumnal days when the foliage is just turning and the walnuts and funghi and white soft cheeses are coming down from the mountains to the markets in the Rialto and Santa Maria Formosa. You see him with different eyes – in the Academy, in the Madonna dell' Orto, in San Giovanni in Bragora – after you have seen Treviso, with its willow-lined river, where the crayfish live, and the exposed little mountain villages near the First World War battlefronts of Monte Grappa and the Piave. His set-jawed throning Virgin looks at you aslant, with the slightly hard, considering stare of a sharp peasant woman; his shaggy Baptists and curly-headed young male saints are herdsmen; and his squinty musician angels are cross-eyed.

How does one recognize Venetian painting? By a brilliance of colour, some say (Antonello's secret); by a greater luminosity, say others (the light of the lagoons). By the subject matter, many would confess, meaning the milky-breasted goddesses, with pearls braided in their gold coiffures, of Titian, Tintoretto, and Veronese, or the views of Guardi and Canaletto. I would say that it identifies itself – and it is always unmistakable – by an enhanced reality, a reverence for the concrete world.

The Venetian merchants were familiar with the feel of stuffs, brocades and silks and damasks, long before there was a Venetian school. These rich materials are one aspect of the continuity of Venetian painting. Starting with Salome's fur and Santa Clara's striped cloak or the gold ribbon-rosettes of Jacobello del Fiore, the show of dress goods goes on through Bellini, Giorgione, Titian, and Veronese, straight up to that theatrical warehouse patronized by Tiepolo for his floats in the sky. Florentine madonnas wear transparent veils and genteel 'old stuffs' – faded blues and old roses with dulled gold trim – that have been handed down for generations in a miserly Tuscan family. This will not do for the Venetians. *Their* madonnas and St Lucys and St Catherines are dressed in brandnew materials fresh from the bolt – expensive figured damasks and cut velvets and olive-green and vermilion silks. No Venetian saint or secular figure is permitted to dress drably. A peasant girl being led into the morning room of a Longhi periwigged gentleman wears little pointed satin shoes with pink buckles that are as high in fashion as St Ursula's little blue bedroom slippers. Striped silver brocades, crimson velvets, cream-coloured and ivory satins, yellow and salmon taffetas, pure-white camlets, pale-blue watered silks – Venetian painting from beginning to end is a riot of dress goods.

The parade of fashion is accompanied by a parade of pets. Birds have always been popular with the Venetians (as they are with prisoners); you see them today, taking the sun in their cages on the vine-covered balconies, *altane*, and archways of the back streets and in the loggias of the palaces on the Grand Canal. In the archway I walk under every day, near San Zaccaria, ten caged birds are swinging. These pet birds are a regular feature of Venetian painting. The most famous are Carpaccio's in 'The Courtesans' – the two fat hot women have an aviary on their *altana*. A falcon appears on a gentleman's wrist in 'The Story of St Ursula.' There is a boy with a bird on the balcony in the well-known Veronese in the Villa Maser. Titian's Mary has a pet bird in the 'Annunciation' in the Scuola di San Rocco. On the steps of Cima's 'Presentation,' next to the basket of eggs that also appears in Titian's, there is a cage full of birds. A Bellini Madonna, in the Duomo of Bergamo, has a dove sitting in a rough, strawy basket that looks ready for the market.

This realism, this suggestion of a domestic intimacy, is what distinguishes the Venetian painters. Tintoretto gave San Rocco a spaniel. St Jerome's dog was a favourite w h Carpaccio; he reappears, riding in a gondola, in 'The Miracle of the True Cross' in the Academy. St Ursula's little dog is waking up on her bedroom carpet as the angel enters. Three dogs are rambling around, reconnoitring, in 'The Marriage Demand.' The dog in the Veronese 'Last Supper' has already been mentioned, but the Inquisitors cannot have looked closely, for in fact there are two. 'The Courtesans' have two dogs to divert them in their stuporous idleness, if indeed that strange creature, resembling an ant-eater, in the left-hand corner is a dog.

But Carpaccio has a whole zoo – deer, camels, pheasants, as well as dogs, lions, dragons, and basilisks. All of these animals appear to be tame. This is true, too, of the Bellini animals. The exotic giraffes, dromedaries, and lions of the Bellini Easter legends are no more terrifying than the lambs, oxen, and rabbits of the Veneto landscapes, or than the straw-eating hippopotamus, an eighteenth-century wonder, painted by Longhi, that hangs in the Ca' Rezzonico.

All birds and beasts, wild and domesticated, are dear to the Venetian painters. Plovers and pheasants, peacocks and partridge, heron and marsh fowl honour Our Lady in Antonio da Negroponte (the 'Throning Madonna' in San Francesco della Vigna), in Mansueti's 'Flight into Egypt,' in Tintoretto. Tintoretto is fondest of wading birds, in low dark ponds and reedy streams; they are present in his San Rocco 'Nativity' beside the Bethlehem stable. Titian likes white rabbits; Veronese's Renaissance ruffed gentleman fancy greyhounds and high-bred hunting dogs. Carlo Crivelli has a wonderful fly that might have come out of an eighteenth-century still life or an entomological slide.

Crivelli is fond of adding cucumbers to the china-like, glazed fruit and flower decorations that surround his Madonnas. A homely realism mingles naturally with high fashion in Venetian art. The bald, sun-bronzed head of an apostle reflects the light from a gold and alabaster jar carried by the Magdalen. Those rugged, swart, bald-headed, old fisher apostles, with their coppery shoulders, are as emblematic of Venetian painting as the sensuous, pensive madonnas with whom they fraternize. The unworldly saints – St Francis, St Aloysius, St Anthony with his lily – are found far less often than the hardy patriarchs. The somewhat cloying Alvise Vivarini is the only Venetian to make a speciality of this kind of subject. The soldier saints, San Marziale, St Martin of Tours, San Liberale, and the early bishops of the church, in glittering robes and mitres, were more in demand.

The paradox of luxury linking arms with utility and beauty with brawny toil was no paradox to the Venetians, who combined palace and warehouse in a single dwelling. It would be false to say that Venetian painting embodied a democratic tendency, and yet that is the impression made on me by Giovanni Bellini, Cima, the Bastiani, Basaiti, and – later – Tintoretto. The company of saints appears as a community of equals, sandalled pioneers of a model Republic, whose women folk could afford the latest styles in dress. This is a republic which includes the animal kingdom – an ark, you might say.

Authority is absent or dispersed among the citizenry. God is 'contained' in heaven, like the doge in his palace. The love of *this* world is a great leveller, as democratic, acquisitive societies all demonstrate. This *pax Venetiana* that descended on painting was never quite broken. The concerts of Giorgione and Titian are translations, into a dreamy Renaissance idiom, of a universal concord. Palma Vecchio's Santa Barbara (in Santa Maria Formosa), with her strong bare toes is a militant citizeness-martyr. Veronese has a wonderful virago, a handsome Mme Defarge, in his 'Martyrdom of St Mark and St Marcilian' in the church where he is buried – San Sebastiano. Titian's bald St Mark – on the ceiling of the Salute sacristy – is still a staunch pillar of an uncorrupted commune. And Tintoretto's whole gigantic effort in the Scuola di San Rocco is to translate the Bible into a stupendous *ordinary* reality that would include all classes, degrees and species in its sweep.

Venetian painting remained hale, like the artists, till an advanced age. It is full of fancy but never morbid. The two morbid painters, Crivelli and Lotto, left robust, high-living Venice and ended their days as wanderers, in the Marches. There is no distortion in Venetian art, despite much ingenuity. The Venetians (like the Americans) hated the idea of death, all through the Renaissance, which elsewhere was half in love with it. The skull appears rarely in Venetian Renaissance art; in fact, I cannot remember seeing one. The absence of fanaticism in Venetian life, the prevalence of mundane motives in politics are reflected in the concreteness, the burnished order and sanity of Venetian painting.

Jacob Burckhardt tells a story of a Venetian merchant

who was present at one of Savonarola's Auto-da-Fés. He
watched them make a great pyramid of objects to be
burned: false hair and beards, scents and toilet articles,
mirrors, chessboards, playing cards, lutes and harps,
volumes of Latin and Italian poets, among them Petrarch
and Boccaccio, and finally two tiers of paintings, chiefly of
beautiful women. When the pyramid was ready, he
offered 22,000 florins for the lot. The Florentines refused,
commissioned his portrait to be painted on the spot, and
burned it with the rest.

The story, I suppose, is basically anti-Venetian: that
merchant had no soul, it might be argued – only an organ
of cupidity. But the organ of cupidity, according to the
old authorities, is precisely the eye. David looked on
Bathsheba and lusted, like the elders on Susanna – a
favourite theme with the Venetians. If there is some
mystery in the fact of a business civilization's producing
generation after generation of incomparable artists, it
lies perhaps in this 'eye,' greedy for materials, for a bargain, but true as a jeweller's lens.

7

Col Tempo

The Venetians invented the income tax, statistical science, the floating of government stock, state censorship of books, anonymous denunciations (the Bocca del Leone), the gambling casino, and the Ghetto. The idea of a Suez Canal was broached by Venice to the sultan in 1504. They were quick to hear of new inventions and discoveries and to grasp their practical application. When the news came to Venice, in 1498, of Vasco da Gama's voyage, rounding the Cape of Good Hope, the whole city instantly understood that it was bad news for their commerce: 'the worst piece of information that we could ever have had.' The telescope, which was invented in Holland in 1608, was known about in Venice before the end of the year. In 1610, it was being tried out from the Campanile, and a Venetian swindler was able to palm off a fraudulent one (made of plain glass) on the Grand Duke of Tuscany.

A Venetian doctor, Salamon, in 1649, anticipated biological warfare by concocting a plague-quintessence for use in the Turkish war. It was to be sown in the enemy's camps through the medium of cloth goods of the type the Turks liked to buy – Albanian fez, for instance. 'The proposition is a virtuous one,' wrote the Venetian *prov-veditore* in Zara to the Inquisitors of State. 'It is however ... unusual and perhaps not admitted by public morality. But ... in the case of the Turks, enemies by faith, treacherous by nature, who have always betrayed your excellencies, in my humble opinion the ordinary considerations have no weight.' The Ten were interested in the proposition and, to make sure of a monopoly on the doctor and his jar of plague-quintessence, they put both of them in jail. In the event, as it seems, the invention may not have been used, possibly because the germs had gone stale – a criticism levelled at the contents of the poison-cupboard in the Doge's Palace when it was checked in the eighteenth century. The Ten were always ready to listen to any ingenious person with a sure-fire scheme, to a murderer who offered to kill the king of Spain for 150 ducats, ex-clusive of travelling expenses, to a forger who guaranteed that he could forge in all languages ...

The *altane* or roof terraces, now chiefly used for hanging out laundry, were a Venetian invention in the field of beauty. The Venetian ladies used to steep their hair in a chemical solution, and sit out on their *altane*, constructed for the purpose, in open-crowned hats, with the hair pulled through and spread out on the brim to bleach in the sun. Hence the golden tresses of Venetian painting. A little of that bleach seems to linger in the Venetian water-supply, for though the Venetians today are not, on the whole, blond, they are not brunette either, but dark with blonde highlights. They have kept the fair skin too that the wide-brimmed hat shielded.

The Venetians first developed the glass mirror commercially in the Murano glass works. They held a monopoly of the art for over a century during the Renaissance. Any mirror-maker who took his art into a foreign state could have his nearest relations imprisoned, and Venetian agents were commissioned to kill him on sight. As late as the seventeenth century, Colbert, Louis XIV's minister, used poison and women to keep certain Venetian mirror-makers in France, and on his death a Venetian mirror, measuring 42 by 26 inches, was found among his effects and inventoried at nearly three times the price of a Raphael.

The *zoccoli*, a bizarre form of footwear, like a mule on a pedestal, were developed in Venice. Originally devised to keep the feet out of the mud, they became one of the wonders of Venice because of the lengths to which they were carried by the love of fashion; a pair preserved in the Correr Museum is twenty inches high. The women wearing them seemed to be walking about on jewelled and brocaded stilts. It is thought that they may have contributed to domestic virtue during the late Middle Ages and early Renaissance, since a lady could not go out without two servants to hold her up. Ordinary shoes would doubtless be more convenient, acknowledged the doge in a conversation with the French ambassador. 'Yes, far, far too convenient,' one of his councillors interposed. Thus even fashion in Venice was converted to practical use. Another suspicion attaching to the *zoccoli* was that the Venetian women wore them to conceal their shortness of stature. 'The Piazza San Marco,' wrote a mainland Italian, 'seems to be full of dwarfs transformed into giantesses.'

But Venice's most wonderful invention – that of the easel-painting – was designed solely for pleasure. Painting, up to Giorgione, had a utility basis: the glorification of God and the saints, the glorification of the state (in the pageant picture), the glorification of an individual (the portrait). Giorgione was the first to create canvases that had no purpose beyond sheer enjoyment, the production of agreeable moods, as Berenson puts it. They were canvases for the private gentleman, for the house, both new conceptions that rested on a new premise: the existence of leisure.

Leisure was the *sine qua non* of the full Renaissance. The feudal nobility, having lost its martial function, sought diversion all over Europe in cultivated pastimes: sonneteering, the lute, games and acrostics, travel, gentlemanly studies and sports, hunting and hawking, treated as arts. Venice did not have a feudal nobility; nor did it have a court, like those of Mantua and Ferrara, where the Renaissance ideal was fixed in patterns that the rest of the world copied. But the decline of Venetian trade, following the discovery of the new trade routes, produced the same results as the break-up of feudalism. The Venetian merchants withdrew their capital from their warehouses and invested it in banking and in *terra ferma* real estate. The Venetian palazzi became mere noble residences, calculated to astonish by their sumptuous decorations. The bales of spices and bolts of cloth that had once filled their entrance halls vanished, and the patrician owners began to build for themselves those pleasurable country 'retreats,' the enchanting gold and white villas of the Veneto, with their long side-wings and balconies, their carefully planned vistas, embodying a functional notion of idleness, of drawn-out desultory days spent in choice conversation with a coterie of friends. Even here, however, Venetian practicality played its part. The Palladian villas have been described as glorified farmhouses; the colonnaded side-wings often contained offices and granaries, and the *piano nobile* was raised over store-rooms corresponding to the warehouses of the palazzi of the Grand Canal.

Nevertheless, it was the age of the amateur that Giorgione was born into, and his easel-paintings not only lend themselves to connoisseurship, to the taste for forming a collection that is one of the amateur's vocations, but they also depict for the first time, a perfectly leisured world: the grassy reverie world of the '*Concert Champêtre*' or the sleeping Dresden 'Venus' on her red bolster and ivory satin throw.

So thoroughly did Giorgione's dreaming, voluptuous temperament express the age's mirror-image that legend made him a gentleman – the illegitimate son of a Veneto patrician, who had fathered him on a Castelfranco peasant woman. Only a few undisputed Giorgiones exist, and this contributes to the vision of a gifted 'divine' amateur. Like Shakespeare, he is an enigmatic figure who seems deliberately to tantalize by withholding biographical information. Almost nothing is known, for sure, about him except that he studied, with the young Titian, in Giovanni Bellini's studio, that he did work, now lost, for the Doge's Palace, that he did frescoes, all but erased by time, for the Fondaco dei Tedeschi, and that he died (of the plague, it is thought) at the age of about 32. Legend relates that he played sweetly on the lute and used to frequent the battlemented castle of the Queen of Cyprus in Asolo, where the Noviates of Love – as described by Cardinal Bembo, who was one of their number as a young man – discussed Platonic affection while they strolled back and forth among the laurel trees and the vine-covered pergolas, listening to the lute and the viol.

Platonic affection! Caterina Cornaro, a dumpy little gopher-faced lady in her portraits, was the pathetic victim of a series of shams. Browbeaten by the Republic into returning the meaningless crown of Cyprus which the Republic had thrust upon her, she was invited (i.e., forcibly retired) to the hill-town castle with the empty title of 'Lady of Asolo' and a court of eighty serving men and twelve maids of honour. She was allowed a favourite negress, who kept her parrots for her, a dwarf buffoon, hounds, apes, and peacocks. The occupations of this imitation court (which is more Veronese than Giorgione), as described by Bembo, give off an aura of heat and deadly, restless tedium, the tedium of an unemployed queen and a train condemned to pleasure. It is the same glazed tedium that emanates, like a scent of stale cosmetics, from the *altana* of 'The Courtesans,' who had their blackamoor and their private menagerie too.

The Platonizing gentleman and maids singing madrigals had nothing else to do. There is a new melancholy in the chronic leisure – which was simply mass unemployment – of the Renaissance nobility. It suffuses Giorgione's paintings, a breath of unrest that just fails to stir the foliage of the trees. Giorgione's works are moody, but I would not say that it was an 'agreeable' mood they created; disturbing, disquieting, rather, they seem to me. It is the absolute fixity of his scenes that makes this strange impression.

Many people feel that there is some mystification in Giorgione, and a group of critics now contends that his work contains a code message designed to be read by a hermetic circle of initiates. Yet there is just one message that Giorgione has written out, placing it in the hand of the old woman of '*La Vecchia*': two words, '*Col Tempo.*' This is usually taken to be a conventional motto, on the order of *Tempus fugit*, or, considerably stronger, a warning to youth and beauty in the mood of Ronsard's '*Quand vous serez bien vieille, au soir, à la chandelle . . .*' I agree with Berenson in feeling that this old, shawled woman with her hand pointing to her shrunken breast is a warning, though I wonder whether it was directed to a particular person (as

he thinks) or to everyone, universally. Warnings must
have been in the air, for this was a dire period. Venice
danced, but the plague was at the door, and the disastrous
war of Cambrai was being fought on the mainland.
Around Vicenza, the pre-Palladian villas built by leisured
humanists to house Platonic Academies were being destroyed by French and German soldiery. Refugees poured
into Venice, including those Jews who were soon shut up
in the Ghetto. The war meant a food shortage and children
were crying for bread on the streets. All observers noted
Venetian indifference to these terrible events. This was the
time when Venice earned the title conferred on her later
by Byron: 'the revel of the earth, the masque of Italy.' The
carnival went on; they called for madder music, stronger
wine. But the old woman was waiting, with her message
clutched in her hand.

No doubt this is too fanciful, but all theories about
Giorgione, like theories about Shakespeare, fall between
two stools – story-telling or deciphering.

In any case, Time is not flying in most of Giorgione's
paintings. Quite the opposite; it seems to have stopped forever at a single moment: in the Castelfranco 'Madonna,'
in '*La Tempesta*,' in the '*Tramonto*,' in the 'Laura,' in 'The
Three Philosophers,' and in '*La Vecchia*' itself – in all the
paintings, in fact, that are considered almost incontestably
Giorgione's. But this dazed sense of arrested time is
precisely a symptom of idleness, of the half-causeless ennui
that is generated by long afternoons in country villas, where
games or music are proposed 'to while the time away.'

The stoppage of time in Giorgione has a partly idyllic character. But the idyll is charged with presentiment, another symptom of *accidia*. This presentiment is in '*La Tempesta*,' which used to be called 'The Soldier and the Gypsy' – in the lurid light and dangerous stillness of the moment in the centre of a storm when the elements seem to pause as if to gather their forces. A jagged streak of lightning darts across the greenish sky, yet in the foreground a kind of false sunlight illuminates a peaceful scene. The red-jacketed, lissom soldier, posed at attention like a herald, the naked gipsy woman, the nursing baby, the green water in the river under the wooden bridge are all absolutely still, as if unaware of the forces that are about to be unleashed on them.

Something frightening is about to happen – this is the suggestion of the painting, which glues the spectator to the spot, just as the curious group is rooted to the landscape. Yet this is the oddest part; they are not rooted but seem to have been put there by hazard. 'Who are they?' 'What are they doing there?' The current school of art criticism discourages such questions; you are expected to look at this startling scene simply from a chromatic point of view. But a Giorgione always *disturbs*. The man and the woman are a queerly assorted pair, and a great distance separates them. Is he her betrayer or has he been sent to guard her? Against what? His handsome profile betrays nothing; he is an attitude, a stance. But the woman's eyes are on you, unmoving, like an arraignment; her swollen belly and the suckling child strike a sombre note of reality in the phantas-

magoric setting. There is an asp-bite to the picture. 'This
is your handiwork,' the woman's body and unflinching
eyes seem to say. To the onlooker? To the gallant soldier?
The presentiment detaches itself from the storm poised
overhead and by a mysterious inversion attaches itself to
the past: something frightening *has* happened and is fixed
forever – that is the painting's second suggestion.

An infinite duration, yet not even a moment has passed,
only the fraction of time that it takes a bolt of lightning to
flash across the sky.

The basilisk look in the eyes of the gipsy becomes even
more ominous in the peculiar, bright, narrowed, confronting stare in the eyes of '*La Vecchia*,' who wears a
white fringed shawl over a baggy pink dress with an
undergarment showing. Her clothing is a mere bundle
over her slack, unsexed frame; a wisp of grey hair hangs
out of her cap against her brown cheek. Reality here, as in
the nursing gipsy, has the character of an inveterate
hostility.

A hypnotic relation between the subject and the spectator is established in all Giorgione's pictures. This derives
partly from the motionless, arrested scene, and partly from
the unwavering look in the eyes of the portrait subjects.
No painter is as transfixing as Giorgione. The stillness
produces the unrest. You look *into* the depths of a Rembrandt old woman, but *La Vecchia* stares into you. Even in
his most tranquil arcadian paintings, the Castelfranco
'Madonna' and 'The Three Philosophers' (where, in each
case, the eyes of the principal figures are averted from the

spectator), something odd in the grouping of the figures produces a sort of inquietude or lingering wonder. The sense of a suspended time inspires questions. 'What is going on here?' you demand of 'The Three Philosophers' or of the tiny pair of armoured figures on the greensward, behind the Madonna's robe in the Castelfranco 'Madonna.' You would never think of asking this question of a very similar group in a Giovanni Bellini. In a Bellini, it would be perfectly clear, self-explanatory in terms of the Bellini commune, where the knight is riding, because that is his business, just as the hermit is fasting and the ploughman is leading his oxen home. The Bellini world is pursuing its gentle course, according to the natural rhythms, whereas the Giorgione world has stopped, leaving a host of queries echoing in the air.

If it is true that Giorgione loved music and was gifted at it (like so many Venetians), this may explain the baffling presence of a time-dimension in his painting. Such pictures as the Castelfranco 'Madonna,' resembling a stately motet, and the '*Tramonto*' have a peculiar reson-ance, like that of a stringed instrument, which continues to vibrate after the last note has been plucked. Giorgione's contemporaries and the immediately succeeding gener-ations found no perplexities in his works. Isabella d'Este, the marchioness of Mantua, wrote to Venice immediately on hearing of Giorgione's death to ask if she could buy 'a night scene, *molto bella e singolare*.' This picture is thought to be '*La Tempesta*,' and *singolare* in all probability meant *rare, exceptional, excellent*. Vasari, the first authority, speaks only of beauty and truth to Nature in Giorgione. The nineteenth century found in him the melancholy of all transitory things, still an agreeable mood. The enigma in Giorgione has slowly come to the surface, like invisible writing held up to the fire. But even today a leading critic talks of the 'profound humanity' of *La Vecchia*, as though she were a Rembrandt. This glittering, toothless hag is soulless, like nearly all Giorgione's people. In spite of their beauty and hypnotic charm (and not all are beautiful; some, like the 'Laura,' fascinate by their ugliness), they are mortals who have lost their souls to the fairies and are punished by living forever.

The prevailing belief about Veronese is that he expressed 'the Venetian joy in life.' The vast banquet scenes and the classical myths and apotheoses support this view, even when they are perfunctory or when the joy in life appears somewhat coarsened and brutalized as in the fat, swollen, cunning faces of the carousers in the 'Banquet of the House of Levi.' Veronese's church, San Sebastiano, painted entirely by his hand, is certainly a joyous church, with its gay convoluted feigned pillars, like Maypoles, its dazzling perspective effects, painted organ-doors, and airy blues and whites. It is a church full of light and music; you expect the organ-doors to fly open and a *Jubilate* to ring out.

In the Doge's Palace and the Academy, the Veronese troop, including many of the Immortals, is greedy, vital, sensual, what people call pagan. Indeed, the first impression is one of a tumultuous rabble of vulgar parvenu persons who have taken possession of a series of classical palaces and who, drunk with success, are invading the sky, being hoisted up onto billowing white clouds in a sort of scaling operation. It is magnificent, overdressed, and appalling.

But there are two Veronese dominions. One is ruled by a fat woman who looks rather like the Empress Maria Theresa. The other is ruled by a young woman with a delicate pensive face and an intent, halted, listening expression. The first may be found in the 'Triumph of Venice' in the Doge's Palace; the second, in the Academy in 'Venice and Hercules and Ceres.' These two women keep reappearing in Veronese's paintings, in Venice, in the Veneto, in all the great collections of the world, sometimes as Venus, sometimes as Europa, sometimes as St Catherine, sometimes as allegorical figures, Industry, Plenty, Harmony. But, whatever their official titles, these joint monarchs – the jowled empress and the fair, thoughtful young queen – are always Venice in her dual aspect.

The first, dominated by the hefty empress in all her finery, is the Venice of splendid entertainments: water pageants and all-women regattas, fantastic barges, the Bucintoro, allegorical representations, crimson velvets, and sky-blue silks. This is the Venice that greeted Henry III of France on his famous visit in 1574, when Veronese was at the height of his powers. Triumphal arches designed by Palladio and painted by Tintoretto were put up as if at a World's Fair. The king was lodged at the Ca' Foscari (now the seat of the university) on the Grand

Canal; it had been specially decorated for him with cloth
of gold and tapestries, a great chimney-piece of precious
marbles, a black marble table with a green velvet cloth, a
ceiling of blue cloth sown with stars, bed sheets
embroidered with gold thread and crimson silk. Paintings
by Giovanni Bellini, Titian, Paris Bordone, Tintoretto
and Veronese hung on the walls. The king's bedroom had
gold and green brocade hangings, a gilded bed with cur-
tains of crimson silk, and an alabaster table. He was given
a banquet in the Hall of the Great Council with three
thousand guests present and a second banquet in the same
room at which the knives, forks, bread, tablecloths, and
napkins were all of sugar, and ornamental statues of popes,
kings, doges, deities, arts, virtues, planets, animals,
flowers, fruit, and trees were made of sugar too, from the
designs of Sansovino, executed by a druggist.

According to Horatio Brown, 'the king never forgot it
nor recovered. His life after was a long mad dream.' The
king's dream (a protracted nightmare following on a
series of heavy banquets and doubtless other fleshly indul-
gence not recorded) had its sequel for the Venetians: an
awakening, tinctured with melancholy, in the candid
morning light of the lagoons. The awakening is also
chronicled by Veronese. That is the second Venice, the
Venice of the young queen with her pure, open brow,
faintly puckered, often, as though a frown would cross it.
Sometimes the frown deepens, as in the 'Industry' or the
'Harmony' of the Villa Maser. Sometimes the young
girl's face is half averted and she appears to be listening,

reflectively, to a sound just heard and pondering its mean-ing. Sometimes she turns into a chained fury as in the 'Vice in Chains to Virtue,' of the same Villa Maser. But wherever this young girl appears, with her simple hair-dress and her slender, circleted neck, there is visible a struggle for meaning.

A look of her still lingers in the Tiepolo 'Venice Wedded to Neptune' in the Doge's Palace.

But if there are two queens in Veronese, there are also two sets of courtiers: the one gross and worldly, swollen and pendulous; the other, grave, thoughtful, with dark curled hair and ruff and pointed beard – the young girl's councillor, wiser and sadder than she. Such a gentleman is the huntsman with his hound and hunting equipment who is just entering the bedroom of the Villa Maser. Here in this columned and voluted pleasure-villa, designed by Palladio, and set in a graceful expanse in the hills near Asolo, is the fullest expression of the 'other' Veronese, depicted in a series of incomparable, haunting frescoes.

They are supposed to express the 'joy in life' of the Venetian leisured country gentlefolk, in this case the Barbaro family, a distinguished Venetian house. But to me they are profoundly sad, to the point, almost, of desper-ation. The young huntsman, in *trompe-l'œil*, entering his bedroom with his dog and his gay accessories, has a look so deep, so quivering, that tears seem to stand in his brilliant, reflective eyes. At the other end of the house, past a long vista of frescoed chambers, his wife, in *trompe-l'œil*, stands facing him in her bedroom door. But the distance is too great; an ordinary, prettyish woman, she does not see the melancholy in her husband's gaze.

The collaboration between Palladio and Veronese is thought to have had a great influence on Veronese's development, adding an architectural dimension to his vast sense of space. In Maser, fresco and architecture pun back and forth on each other. *Trompe-l'œil* mimics architectural elements; startling, lifelike dwarfs open false doors; the long balconies missing from the palace façade are supplied in fresco in the interior. The simulated balcony (always dear to Veronese for the tiers of space it permitted) has a unique purpose at Maser. The residents of the house – the lady herself, Signora Barbaro, in a blue-and-silver dress, and the old nurse – are shown on a balcony looking down into an octagonal room, turned around, that is, where in real life they would be looking outward, down the long broad walk with its flanking low wall, topped by small statues, to the road and the ordered fields beyond. This outward look, as of people expecting company, turned down upon the room, gives the peculiar intentness that is characteristic of Veronese. Across from this balcony, there is a second one, on which two boys are shown, in profile, one with a book, like a young Hamlet, the other with a bird. They are intent too and preoccupied, oblivious of the two women scanning them from the opposite balustrade. The effect, so lively, so lifelike, is, in the small room, inexplicably sad. It is a stage house inside a real house – an idea that sounds sportive and playful, a mirror trick, but that is too well executed to be amusing, like the sort of game where the children playing it work themselves up till they begin to cry.

Between the *trompe-l'œil* apparitions, myths and allegories in pale lovely fresco colours, brightened by an occasional leaf-green ribbon, are painted on the walls and ceilings. But these are not usual pagan decorations. The Olympians are not disporting themselves in riotous abandon. They are engaged in some serious task that commands all their attention. The grave young women frown, like dancers or musicians concentrating on a difficult performance. Some figures regard each other; some stare straight ahead; now and then, from underneath a diadem, a pair of eyes flashes a fierce, baleful look downward into the salon.

This house is full of eyes; that is the curious impression. It is very different from Giorgione. These natures have the capacity, not only to watch, but to feel passion and suffer. Idyllic or arcadian, Maser certainly is not. But it is beautiful and moving. The dead figures on the walls seem almost terrifyingly alive. It is a kind of animal life, quick, alert, and prescient, the intelligent, higher side of the bestiality represented in the carnivorous banquets. The combination of thoughtfulness and animal vitality – the Renaissance tragic paradox – is what makes Veronese, for me, at Maser and now everywhere, the greatest of Venetian painters. This, in the end, was Ruskin's view, though he did not have the same reasons.

It is the eternal Venetians who crowd the Veronese balconies, a lively people, but not especially joyous. Curious, attentive, courteous, slightly sad – so they are now and so, in their ensemble, I think they were in Veronese's day. He was the only one among the artists of the Golden Age to show the ensemble, and his scenes have a marked resemblance to the Elizabethan stage: grossness and delicacy; Falstaff, on the one hand, Hamlet, on the other; Juliet and the Nurse.

8

Finale

Titian's last picture, finished by Palma Giovane, is a *Pietà* in the Academy. The fellow-pupil of Giorgione was by then 99 years old, according to the traditional belief, now questioned by modern scholars, who whittle the figure down to 91 or even 86. This painting, done in the grave's shadow, is appropriately set in a tomb. The plague was again in Venice, in Titian's own house, at the time he began the painting. The following year, Palladio started building the pink Church of the Redentore on the Giudecca, one of the five plague-churches in Venice, erected on five different occasions in thanksgiving for relief from the scourge. A premonition (natural enough) of his end must have visited Titian, for he intended the '*Pietà*' for his own tomb in the Frari. The plague took him, before he had finished it, in 1576, sixty-six years after it had taken Big George of Castelfranco. The Holy Sepulchre in the painting is a rich Renaissance niche, framed with neoclassical pedestals and lions. An emblem of the phoenix is set over the grave in which Christ's body is about to be deposited. An angel (resembling a cupid) is descending with a torch. Another *Pietà* – a picture within a picture – is shown in one corner. In short, the trappings are conventional Renaissance. Yet a tragic passion springs out of it. The Mother in a brown veil and blue mantle makes a chill, severe contrast with the glowing Titian flesh tones. A Magdalen, in a green robe, like an Avenging Angel, is turning away from the grave-scene with upraised arm, confronting the spectator with a look of *terribilità*. This is a piercing, frenzied cry, the most fearsome expression of the mood in Venetian painting that began with the ambiguous idyll of Giorgione. Coming as it does, at the end of a long comfortable career of worldly success and international fame, that disordered Magdalen is like a Gorgon or like the Erinyes howling at the old man's door. These sudden confrontations (first seen perhaps in the Torcello Madonna), these demands, so to speak, for a reckoning or ultimate meaning, pass out of Venetian painting with the death of Veronese.

Titian was a world figure, the darling of the pope and of the Emperor Charles V. It is logical, therefore, that only scraps of his work should remain in Venice, the enemy of the Curia and of the Spanish power. There is really very little and that not of the first quality: a 'Venus' in the Ca' d'Oro, the 'Presentation' in the Academy, the Frari 'Assumption' and 'Madonna with the Pesaro family,' a head of St Mark in the Salute sacristy, the uncompleted painting in the Doge's Palace, an 'Annunciation' in the Scuola di San Rocco, a St Lawrence in the strange *trompe-l'œil* church of the Gesuiti, where the Venetian love of rich materials and optical illusions has been carried to bizarre lengths by the Jesuit fathers and the whole interior, down to a fake carpet, is covered with marbles counterfeiting brocade. Again, it seems logical that the Jesuits, themselves the pets of the Emperor and odious to the Venetians, should own one of the few examples of Titian in Venice. The Frari 'Assumption,' moreover, though owned by the Franciscans, is quite in the Jesuit taste. Ruskin detested it, rightly, I think; with its gaudy reds and blues, it seems to be the first sample of that religious propaganda art which the Jesuits used to 'sell' the faith to the masses.

To see Titian in Venice is to conceive an unfair prejudice against him – the great Titians are in the Prado, Naples, and the Louvre – yet hardly any visitor is immune to this experience. The old rivalries among the Venetian painters of the Golden Age flare up hotly again in the churches, *scuole*, and museums. Tintoretto is preferred to Titian; Titian and his blackmailing friend, that monster of vanity, Aretino – who wrote that he saw his likeness everywhere in Venice, in majolica ware, on the façades of *palazzi*, on comb-boxes and mirror-ornaments 'like a Scipio or Alexander' – are held responsible for the exile of Lotto, whose Carmine altarpiece was satirized by a hack writer and hanger-on of the Sansovino-Titian-Aretino log-rolling company, as Berenson calls it. Titian's jealousy of the young Tintoretto is cited; the story is told that Titian, envying the Little Dyer's drawing, excluded him from his studio. The Venetians plume themselves on Titian, a provincial from Cadore, but it is hard not to feel, on their behalf, that in some sense he betrayed the Republic, with his Florentine friends and the pope and the Spanish Emperor.

Most visitors to Venice fall in love with Tintoretto or they 'discover' him here for the first time, which amounts to the same thing. The syllables 'Tintoretto' must vie with '*il conto*,' as the most commonly pronounced in Venice. He is the one the gondoliers chatter of and the children in the street. St Mark's, the Doge's Palace, the Gothic churches of the Frari and S. Zanipolo, the Rialto, the Grand Canal, a gondola ride, and Tintoretto comprise the touristic Venice. Scarcely a sightseer leaves without a pilgrimage-visit to the Scuola di San Rocco, which houses the 'Crucifixion' series. His wraithlike figures, his staggering perspective arrangements, his diagonals, his chiaroscuro, the whole gigantism of him, make a stupendous, unforgettable impression on the layman, who would be shocked to learn that professional art critics today depreciate his works. He is the literary amateur's painter; torrents of descriptive prose have been expended on him, as though to match his own torrential output.

'Surely, no single picture in the world,' writes Henry James of 'The Crucifixion,' 'contains more of human life; there is everything in it, including the most exquisite beauty . . . There are pictures by the Tintoret which contain touches more exquisite, revelations of beauty more radiant, but there is no other vision of so intense a reality and an execution so splendid.' Further on, however, he

speaks of 'poor dusky Tintoret'; the pictures in the Scuola
were blackened and rotting, and the average person,
James says, in the dim room, would get a sense of 'the
genius loci having been a sort of mad whitewasher, who
worked with a bad mixture, in the bright light of the
campo, among the beggars, the orange-vendors, and the
passing gondolas.'

Since that time, the paintings have been cleaned, lights
have been installed, and the average person, including me,
reacts with due respect. Tintoretto is certainly inferior to
the great Venetians – Carpaccio, Bellini, Cima, Giorgione,
Veronese, Titian. He is perhaps even what the critic
Longhi calls him: 'the Stakhanovite of the Scuola di San
Rocco.' But the force of this genius takes the breath away.
One's admiration is given more, possibly, to the *conception*
of a Tintoretto than to its realization. He writes large what
he means to convey; that is why we amateurs respond to
the 'terrific' effects of 'The Last Supper,' 'The Crucifixion,'
'The Manger,' 'The Annunciation.' We see at once what
he is up to; the unleashing of a supernatural event that
strikes into ordinary life like a cyclone, knocking everything askew, tilting tables and crockery, so that everything seems to be sliding, as in a house carried away by a
wind or a flood. These sliding, dangerous diagonals leave
no doubt as to their intention, which is partly to amaze by
their artistic legerdemain – Tintoretto was a super sales-
man – but also to evangelize.

There is strong evangelical excitement in the Scuola di
San Rocco series, an afflatus of that mood of reformed

Christianity, of direct revelation, that produced the Quakers and Shakers long afterwards in the Anglo-Saxon mercantile communities. This is gospel truth, these paintings seem to preach, pointing to the slightly hairy, snub-nosed peasant girl who is receiving the Annunciation or to the strawy barn in Bethlehem that seems to smell of dung. Even Ruskin, who was enraptured with Tintoretto, found the disciples too vulgar in 'The Last Supper.' But Tintoretto was not concerned with refinement here; he was looking for an effect that would 'tell,' like a minister scanning his congregation in search of some homely example.

The first percussive shock of these San Rocco paintings, followed by a flash of comprehension, makes one gasp. But it is impossible to take them all in. There are too many (fifty-two important ones by Ruskin's count), and the shocks succeed each other with a somewhat deadening regularity. The dynamic ceases to electrify, and one turns to the palmy, peaceful scenes – St Mary of Egypt, sitting under a palm tree, the Magdalen under a laurel tree, 'The Flight into Egypt,' the farmyard in the lower tier of 'The Manger.' All these shady paintings have water in them, the dark pools and streams that Tintoretto loved to show, even in the African desert. St Mary of Egypt is sitting near the river Jordan; she has, by the way, two qualifications for being a Venetian saint – first, she was a courtesan, and, second, when she died, her remains were buried by a pious lion. In any case, the palms, the cool water, the wading birds, the peacock, all these exotic fancies refresh the spectator, who in this gloomy Scuola with its burning message, could forget that he is in Venice. This is the only building in Venice that is claustrophobic.

Tintoretto painted too much; there is no doubt of it. After the first revelation, you tire of this tireless productivity, and of that procession of sacristans crowing 'Tintoretto,' as they lead you into some dark chapel or robing room. Each sacristan believes that his Tintoretto (more often, plural) is a special treat he has for the foreigner; if you pass idly over one of these canvases, he will pluck at your sleeve – 'Tintoretto!' – and urge you back. It is like the cry 'Gondola, gondola' that meets me every day as I cross the Bridge of the Canonica till it comes to seem like an obscene suggestion. Nevertheless, there are many beautiful Tintorettos in Venice, in sinuous contredanse patterns of delicate pinks, blues, and mauves.

Following Tintoretto, Venetian painting, as if exhausted, lay dormant until the eighteenth century. When it awoke, it was to the bright toy Venice of Canaletto and Guardi, to the masquerades of the two Tiepolos, to the delicate spun-sugar figures of Longhi and the stickier candied *genre* of Piazzetta. Venice, in the interval, had become a 'subject,' and thenceforth it sat still as an artist's model for many painters and holders of the pen: Casanova, Rousseau, Lady Mary Wortley Montagu, the Président de Brosses, Goldoni, Byron, Browning, Ruskin, Turner, Bonington, Barrès, Corvo. As a narrative, this becomes a little wearying, for in the eternal carnival Venice nothing ever happens, except 'adventures,' that is, short-lived, dreamlike episodes.

A remarkable fact about this most romantic of all cities is that it has no lovers, no Paolo and Francesca, or Cenci, or even Petrarch and Laura. The Venetian love stories, such as they are, were spun in the brains of foreigners: *Othello, The Merchant of Venice, Il Fuoco, Death in Venice, The Desire and Pursuit of the Whole*. The real, historic lovers whose trysting-places are pointed out – D'Annunzio and Duse, George Sand and Musset, Byron and the Guiccioli – were in Venice as tourists. Byron's friend, Hobhouse, wrote him: 'Be content with your Naiads, your amphibious fry.' He wanted to discourage Byron from following the Countess Guiccioli back to her native Ravenna, where the women were *terra ferma* creatures who made real demands and caused trouble. He was unsuccessful in his argument, for Byron, who was tired of Venice and its mixed bag of sexual opportunities, found a serious, taxing love irresistible.

Promiscuous sex of all kinds was rampant in Venice even in the Middle Ages. In 1443, a law forbidding transvestism was passed; any man found in female dress was liable to a fine. Prostitutes, to attract Venetian men, used to go about in men's clothes. In 1480, a decree published in Latin declared these practices to be a form of sodomy. But nearly a hundred years later, in 1578, two years after the death of Titian, a new ordinance was passed, forbidding courtesans to go through the city in gondolas, *vestite da homo*. Venice has always been *accommodating* sexually, catering to all tastes, like the great hotel it is, with signs in French, German, English, and Italian ('*Petit déjeuner,*'

'*Frühstück*,' '*Breakfast*,' '*Prima colazione*') advertising the mixture-as-before. The Italian institution of the *cicisbeo* (sometimes a lover, sometimes a gigolo, sometimes a mere escort, to a married woman) was perfected, if not invented, in Venice. Here again was Venetian rationality: the signora's goldfish bowl, the Ghetto, the method of electing a doge – a perfect piece of machinery that calls to mind the old limerick: 'Concave or convex, It would fit either sex, And perfectly simple to clean.' Sexual excess reached its peak, probably, in the eighteenth century; it had spread from the sixteenth-century courtesans to married women of all classes.

Yet in all the letters and diaries, there is no word of romance or of disastrous passion – only of gallantry. Casanova had the true Venetian temperament: cool, ebullient, and licentious. It was not a 'warm' city; that warm soul, Jean-Jacques Rousseau, found himself impotent on the two occasions when Venetian prostitutes tried to initiate him. This absence of passion no doubt contributes to the unreal character of Venetian life, which appears as a shimmering surface, like Venetian music. In the traditional Venetian serenades, played from cruising gondolas, the songs today are all Neapolitan. Foreigners cavil at this, but the Venetians point out that there are no love songs in the Venetian repertory – only witty exchanges between man and maiden.

The Venetians were extremely inventive, musically. The

organ was developed in Venice; a native son of the Veneto
made the first violin. The madrigal was invented in
Venice by a Dutchman named Willaert. Galuppi was
born in Burano; the Gabrielis, Vivaldi, and Benedetto
Marcello were born in Venice. Monteverdi was *maestro
di cappella* for many years at St Mark's – one of the great
choirs of Italy, the rival of the *cappella* in Mantua and St
Cecilia's in Rome. Monteverdi, like Cimarosa, died in
Venice. The Venetian passion for music was symbolized by
Sansovino, the Florentine, in his statue of Apollo on the
Loggetta. During the sixteenth century, the most ordinary
parish church had its choir and its organ; flutes were
peddled in the street, like today's glass beads and pigeon
food. Sir Henry Wotton sent a lord of the Privy Council 'a
set of glasses of my own choosing at Murano and some
lutes and strings for your music.'

Indeed, Venetian music has the delicate, fragile sound of
a fork struck on glass. This music – Cimarosa, Galuppi,
Cavalli, Monteverdi, Benedetto Marcello – is still heard
on summer and fall evenings at concerts given in the
court of the tall Ca' Pisani, which is like a Veronese palace,
or in the court of the Palladian San Giorgio Maggiore. The
music played in the Piazza cafés is of rather poor quality;
the Quadri side, which used to be the Austrian side during
the Austrian occupation, now – because Venice is changeless – entertains German tourists with Viennese waltzes and
'*Ach du lieber Augustin.*' For the Americans there is '*A rive-
derci, Roma*... Good-bye, good-bye, good-bye.'

The municipal band plays the usual classical repertory

on a stand in the Piazza several nights a week during the summer and fall. More Venetian are the bell of the Marangona in the Campanile, tolling out the main divisions of day – sunrise, noon, midnight – the bell of the enamelled clock tower, struck every hour by the two giant bronze figures amid a scattering of pigeons, the bells of San Francesco della Vigna sounding over the Laguna Morta. The Venetians recognize all their bells by sound. Their dialect has its own peculiar music, high and sweet, like the chirping of birds.

It has the same lively rhythm as the quick, tapping step, up-and-down, up-and-down, that the Venetians have developed to match the form of their multitudinous bridges, which are seldom thrown straight across the water, but arched, with flights of stairs up and down. The Venetians, when giving directions, do not say 'Across the bridge,' but '*Giù il ponte*' ('Down the bridge").

In the eighteenth century, society went on Sundays to the orphanages to hear the renowned girl-choirs. Some of these orphan soloists were famous as *artistes* while they were still children. Rousseau went to hear them and was disappointed in their looks, which were not as heavenly as their voices. From Venice, he brought back to France his revolutionary musical ideas, just as (he said) he found inspiration for his theory of the Social Contract in the government of the Republic.

But the music floating in the Venetian air, like the sex that still seems to charge it, never deepened into full-throated passion but retained its gossamer virtuosity. Except in painting (the perennial great exception in this city that is all eyes), there are no crashing chords in Venetian life or history. The Campanile, when it fell, is said to have subsided gently, as though making a curtsey. The Republic started declining after the Chioggian War, in 1380, but it took five centuries for the social structure to topple, gently, like the Campanile, which had gone through fire and earthquakes and been struck three times by lightning, and when it fell on Bastille Day morning, 1902 – everything in Venice is an allusion – was found to be nothing but a heap of dust.

The great deeds of Venetian history were over when her art-history began. The war of Chioggia had been finished fifteen years when Jacopo Bellini was born. Venetian painting seems to alternate, like the figures in a Swiss weather clock, with Venetian prowess in the field. When the Lion of War is rampant, the Muse is in retirement. During the seventeenth century, while the Republic's art was dormant, Francesco Morosini, called the Peloponnesian, revived the tradition of Venetian military valour by some short-lived triumphs in Greece. He brought the lions home to the Arsenal – the last of St Mark's thefts – and a triumphal arch, of almost Roman grandiosity, was erected to him in the Doge's Palace. He was one of the few Venetian leaders to receive personal publicity; a series of rooms in the Correr Museum is devoted to the celebration of his exploits, his ancestors, and his wife. But outside of

Venice, his fame rests on the fact that it was under his command that a Venetian shell fell on the Parthenon, which the Turks were using as a powder-magazine. The middle of the temple was blown out and the side-columns fell. Later, in trying to pull down the chariot of Athena, to take home as a trophy, from the west pediment – an unsuccessful attempt – Morosini inflicted further damage on the sculpture. As Marx said, every historical event, having figured once as drama on the stage of history, reappears as farce.

In painting, the Tiepolos, father and son, made an energetic effort to resurrect the Grand Style. Tiepolo was a poet of space,.like Veronese, but he could not take the Veronese world quite seriously, and his frescoed walls and ceilings are a kind of delicate *opéra bouffe* of the Veronese subjects. He worked in the villas of the Veneto, where Veronese had painted, in the Venetian palaces, and in the churches: Sant' Alvise, the Gesuati, Santa Maria della Fava, and the Scalzi, whose ceiling was bombed by the Austrians during the First World War (two pendentives hang in the Academy). The wonderful Tiepolo sky is filled with goddesses, whose round luscious legs and bare feet dangle fetchingly from the clouds. But it is also the scene of a series of grotesque parades, as if the sky were mirroring the somewhat debased regattas on the Grand Canal. Furling crimson banners, poufs of yellow taffeta, Corinthian columns, lions, broken pediments, ladders, spears, and trumpets, Red Indians in feathered headdresses – the Tiepolo parade is a half-barbarian triumph enacted on a sequence of floats. His genius plays the game of how heavy, how encumbered, he can make his sky-chariots while still convincing the beholder that they are lighter than air, and he often loads them with military machinery, even battering-rams. He is utterly successful with this game, this delightful illusion. But a certain revulsion from the charade of 'Glorifications' is manifest in the likenesses he made of the nobles and bishops who paid for these flatteries: these are cruel, thick-lipped, dissipated satyrs' faces, and the laurel crown placed on the swollen triumphal heads comes out in two points, goatishly, like faun's ears. Tiepolo understood the bestial, and the dignitaries of his neo-classic world are often on the verge of some Ovidian metamorphosis, into a lower form of nature, as if their upstart *hubris* had offended a god.

He finished his life in Spain, where his work is thought to have influenced Goya. His son, Giandomenico, yielded himself unreservedly to the spirit of the harlequinade. A picture like 'The New World' in the Ca' Rezzonico, with its long line of figures stumpily facing seaward, while waiting to take their turns in a mountebank's peepshow, is a *reductio ad absurdum* of the old Venetian pageant picture and its stately horizontals. He did rustic subjects in the international taste and grisailles of masked figures and clowns. These clowns of Giandomenico are turned out today in black and white china, as table-ornaments, by the more high-brow Murano glass works.

The clown, the mask, the gondola, the portico, the palace – these are the motifs of the long mad dream of the eighteenth century, crystalline in Canaletto, chequered with noonday sun and deep shadow in Guardi. Canaletto and Guardi are the last, one might say, of the Venetian mirror-makers. Canaletto's mirror is steel and Guardi's is glass, old glass, darkened in streaks and romantically discoloured. The scene they reflect is the changeless Venice of the eighteenth-century memoirs, the city in which nothing ever happens but adventures. The ear tires of this, but the eye does not. No one would complain of Canalettos that they are 'all alike.' This is precisely their point. They please us by repeating, just as a mirror does. The perennial wonder of Venice is to peer at herself in her canals and find that she exists – incredible as it seems. It is the same reassurance that a looking-glass offers us: the guarantee that we are real. In Canaletto and Guardi, the Venetian mirage is affirmed and documented: the masks and the bobbing gondolas, the Rialto Bridge, the Dogana, and the blue curtain of the Salute blowing in a freshened breeze. This art is close to photography, as Venetian literature is always close to journalism, i.e., to the eye-witness report. Now the clowns and the masks are gone, but the umbrella might substitute for them, as a symbol of contemporary Venice – forests, armies of umbrellas, wheeling, defiling, bowing to each other, begging pardon, in the narrow *calli* during the winter rains.

The bizarre line of figures in Giandomenico's painting staring seaward toward a conjectural New World beyond the horizon, while they allow themselves to be diverted by a mountebank, symbolizes the Venetian predicament. It was time for the gondolier's comment, 'At last, he's turned the page.' But the energy had run out. The fresh page remained a blank. It had taken the Venetian patricians five hundred years to spend the capital accumulated during the 'glorious' period; when it was finally dissipated, there was nothing left to live for. Venetian art abruptly collapsed, like a punctured bubble, with the death of the Republic. Giandomenico, the last of the Venetian painters, like his father, died in Spain. The Academy, which had been started by Piazzetta as a sort of painters' society, along the lines of the Royal Academy, with himself and the senior Tiepolo as presidents, was reconstituted as a museum by Napoleon, who was not lacking in a sense of drama. Once again, he closed a story.

Now that the carnival is over, the Venetians have adjusted themselves with a good grace. There are no acrobats any more to slide down a rope on Shrove Tuesday and alight at the doge's feet in the loggia of the Ducal Palace, no bullfights in the Piazza, no Ascension Day fair. But there are still regattas, with the *sestieri* competing, and there is still the bridge of boats thrown across the Giudecca Canal to Palladio's church on the Feast of the Redentore. On the night of the Redentore (the eve of the third Sunday in July) there is a tremendous fireworks display. Boats of all kinds, hung with Chinese lanterns – gondolas, barges, rowboats, a float carrying the orchestra of the Fenice theatre, motorboats, an old Venetian galleon – mass in the dark Giudecca Canal to watch the rockets and Roman candles go off from the Piazzale Roma, near the station. For an hour, the sky is illuminated by bursts of coloured stars; the *palazzi* rock with the explosions; greens and golds, reds and violets are reflected in the water and in the darkened windows of the houses. It is a picture, everyone agrees, or rather a series of pictures; shades of Guardi, of the Bassano night-scenes, even of Carpaccio, pass across the Canal. Everyone seeks for a comparison, and all comparisons seem true: I myself think of the Embarkation of the Queen of Cyprus, in a painting in the Correr Museum. When the fireworks are over, nobody starts for home; a second show (how typical of Venice) is about to begin, the duplicate, the twin, of the first, at the other end of the Canal, on the island of San Giorgio, where the other Palladian church is lit up. All the boats move off in procession, accompanied by music. Traditionally, after the second fireworks display, you are supposed to be rowed to the Lido to see the sunrise. As a gondolier explained to me, gravely, the true colours of nature ('*i veri colori della natura*') refresh the eye after the fires of artifice.

There spoke Venice, the eternal connoisseur, in the voice of her eternal gondolier. The Feast of the Redentore, celebrating relief from the plague, remains the most characteristic Venetian festival. A Feast of Lights that follows, in August, with illuminated floats on the Grand Canal, is a rather drummed-up affair. It is not a specifically

Venetian feast, and the Venetian popular heart is not in it. During Ascension week, in the spring, the three kings in the Clock Tower, accompanied by an angel with a horn, come out, on the hour, and make their bows to the Madonna; in the summer there is the Tombola or Lottery in the Piazza. But above all, for the Venetian delectation, there are the foreigners. The Venetians have been entertaining themselves at our expense, ever since the limping Lord Byron obliged them by swimming the Grand Canal and George Sand in man's clothes stayed at Danieli's with Musset. We are their staple of amusement; it is we who ride in the gondolas and are serenaded at night by American Express. All winter, we keep coming, even during the rainy season, when the Piazza is flooded and planks are laid down from St Mark's atrium and everyone carries an umbrella (since everyone must walk), to the nearest vaporetto stop, for the gondolas no longer solicit business, the *felze* or ornamental covering being inadequate as shelter. The streets bristling with umbrellas in quasi-military formations, make me think of a Venetian admiral's description of the Turkish armada as he came upon it unexpectedly: 'The sea bristled like a pine forest.' Like everything in Venice, winter takes on a fabulous, improbable character; for the travellers who have seen it, it becomes a curiosity, a traveller's tale. Snow in St Mark's Square, St Mark's Square flooded, skating on the canals – these oddities are reported by eye-witnesses and recorded by Venetian painters. The normal looks queer.

'*Che brutto giorno!*' My shrewd, clowning signora

and her family have slowly, like cats, repossessed their apartment, corner by corner, room by room. Hairpins and a hair-dryer have appeared in the bathroom that is supposedly 'mine.' Next, it is nylon underwear hanging in the bathroom window. Mascara and a mascara brush, powder, a comb, have crept, one by one, onto the toilet table. One day, the bathtub is full of laundry. '*Scusi,*' says the signora, pulling one of her most abject faces; it is easier for her, this one time, to do the wash there. '*Lei permette?*' I permit. Now I am lucky if I can get a bath, assuming there is any hot water; the laundry soaking in the bathtub has become a permanent fixture. My toilet soap vanishes, as if by magic. I buy a new cake, and in a day or so it is a sliver. I find I have to buy a fresh box of powder. A guest comes to stay with me, and the signora takes her aside, to ask her, *per piacere,* where she buys her toothpaste. 'Mario *loves* it!' she declares, alluding to her son. Next day, when we meet the signora on the street, a cloud of perfume envelops her which I cannot fail to recognize as my Patou 'Joy.'

As soon as I leave the apartment, the whole family frisks about among my possessions, touching, tasting, sniffing. 'Your glasses exactly fit my eyesight,' confides the signora when I come home after a day out. This naïve candour disarms me. What can I say? '*Dov' è il suo braccialetto?*' demands the signora, in indignant reproach, when I have taken my bracelet to be fixed at the jeweller's. Ransacking my drawers, evidently, she has found it missing and she treats this as if it were a crime on my part, as though I owed it to her not to lose an object that she had refrained from purloining herself. My cleaning fluid disappears; it is these articles connected with the toilet that fascinate the family most, as though my foreign identity were secreted in its quintessence in the tubes, jars, and bottles. They are waiting for me to make some sign of protest, I suppose, but nothing they do, in itself, seems worth making a fuss about. The signora's vegetables and dairy goods invade my icebox. An ironing board is set up in the kitchen. '*Lei permette?*' says the signora. Soon, the entire family, except the Jovian signore, is established around the kitchen table. They no longer go through the formality of offering to leave when I come in with my groceries. The son and daughter of the house stand behind me, watching me cook and commenting, curiously, to each other.

It is their curiosity, I feel, that leads them to try out all sorts of dodges on me – merely to test my reactions. How far will I let them go, they wonder, not with any particular end in view, but to find out how I work. Their whole life seems to be conducted on a similar principle; there is a continuous testing of reality, to see how far it will yield and when it will resist – Venetian experimentation.

One morning, the telephone, which sits on the entrance-hall table, is gone, and I fear that the signora's debts (she is a spendthrift in the old Venetian style) have closed in on her. But no; she has engaged an *operaio privato* to install extra telephone outlets, upstairs in her quarters; in my bedroom; in the kitchen – without the knowledge of the telephone company. A few weeks later, the *operaio privato* is back, to plug up the outlets; the telephone company has somehow found out. For a week, a man comes every day with a chair that he is trying to deliver to the signora, who warns me not to accept it and to say that she has gone away. Indeed, whenever the doorbell rings, the signora materializes on the stairway, her finger to her lips, signalling me not to acknowledge that she is at home. I hear her answering her phone, pretending to be the housekeeper. She looks at me and winks. It is all a game, an experiment.

Strange people are introduced into the apartment with various articles for sale: clothes and trays of jewellery that the vendor, supported by the signora, declares to be gold and diamonds. When I manifest no interest, the signora is not cast down. She shrugs and hustles the vendor out of the house. She has discovered, almost to her satisfaction, the threshold of my tolerance, the point where I balk. But soon she comes back from a week-end with three paintings which she says (confidentially) are de Pisis. Does she expect me to buy them or merely to believe the attribution? Or both? Or neither? When I say nothing, the pictures vanish. The furniture and trappings of the apartment are all in a state of flux – here today, gone tomorrow. Nothing is anchored to its place, not even the coffee-pot, which floats off and returns, on the tide of the signora's marine nature. The pictures change on the walls in a quite hallucinatory fashion. A Tintoretto (*scuola di*) that was looking down at me during the lunch hour by dinner-time is a Giorgionesco. An aura of comic mystery cloaks all her doings. She will never send for a regular *facchino* from the San Zaccaria station; it has to be an *operaio privato*. Yet despite her devious intrigues, the signora is completely transparent. Her long face is a windowpane through which anyone can see her thoughts.

Guilelessly guileful, she is as far as a baby from conceiving the very notion of hypocrisy. All property has a deep attraction for her; yet she has no conception of what property is and is as nonchalant in lending as she is in borrowing. A deception clearly has some function, in the signora's mind, but it is not exactly to command belief. She is an utter realist who lives in a web of unreal schemes and plans that can never come off. '*Ah, pouvera Venezia,*' she cries as she flings open the window in the morning, in the same tone that she cries, '*Ah, povera Elva.*' She is always Venice in her own eyes, fallen on evil days, reduced to living on the foreigner, who will soon go away and leave her. But she does not really care; she is a fatalist.

And I shall have to go soon, I dreamily realize, or I shall come back one day to the apartment and find that *I* have vanished, following my soap and perfume. I shall no longer exist, and the signore and the signora, having swallowed me, will be back, yawning, in the *letto matrimoniale*, beneath the gold cupids, the signora's mermaidtail tucked under her embroidered wedding sheets.

When I go, it will have to be by gondola because I have so much baggage. Some private Charon of the signora's will ferry me down to the station in his shabby funera bark. That is how the Allies took Venice, arriving from the mainland, at the end of the second World War. There was a petrol shortage, and the Allied command, having made secret contact with the gondoliers' co-operative, officially 'captured' Venice with a fleet of gondolas. Even war in Venice evokes a disbelieving smile.

Books by Mary McCarthy
available in paperback editions
from Harcourt Brace Jovanovich, Publishers

The Mask of State

The Seventeenth Degree

Medina

Memories of a Catholic Girlhood

The Writing on the Wall and other Literary Essays

The Company She Keeps

The Stones of Florence

Venice Observed